- Set up interclass special interest groups for enrichment and motivation
- Put together a cooperative class magazine that stimulates student creativity
- Notify parents of a special individual enrichment project

What's more, you'll find new, ready-to-use teaching ideas for complete lessons, long projects, enrichment, games, and activities for all age groups.

You get samples of an original social studies game, a complete programmed booklet, a goal sheet, an interest inventory, a curiosity questionnaire, and a project report.

Here, in short, is a practical, how-to-guide which emphasizes flexibility in grouping and planning so as to meet the needs of the individual AND the teacher.

ABOUT THE AUTHOR

ROSALIND MINOR ASHLEY received her B.A. from Northwestern University, and has done advanced studies at Northeastern University and National College of Education. She has taught for eight years in the Illinois school system, and was an Associate Editor for Scott, Foresman and Company, educational publishers. Mrs. Ashley has contributed articles to *Elementary English, Instructor,* and *Teacher* magazines. Her other books, published by Parker Publishing Company, Inc., include *"Successful Techniques for Teaching Elementary Language Arts"* and *"Activities for Motivating and Teaching Bright Children."*

simplified teaching techniques
and materials ━━━━━━━━━━━━━━━
for flexible group instruction

Simplified Teaching Techniques
and Materials
for Flexible Group Instruction

Rosalind Minor Ashley

Parker Publishing Company, Inc.

West Nyack, New York

©1976 *by*

PARKER PUBLISHING COMPANY, INC.
West Nyack, New York

Library of Congress Cataloging in Publication Data

Ashley, Rosalind Minor.
    Simplified teaching techniques and materials for
flexible group instruction. see slip.

    Includes bibliographical references, and index.
    1. Group work in education. I. Title.
LB1032.A83   371.39   76-792
ISBN 0-13-810093-4

Printed in the United States of America

To my family:
Chuck, Steve, and Rick Ashley,
and Fay and Jack Minor.

Other Books by the Author

Successful Techniques for
Teaching Elementary Language Arts

Activities for Motivating and Teaching
Bright Children

HOW THIS BOOK WILL HELP YOU
TO TEACH WITH FLEXIBLE GROUPINGS _____

This is a problem-solving book to help teachers meet the challenge of individualizing with a roomful of active children. It shows you realistic methods for teaching the large group, the small group, and the individual as efficiently as possible. It provides suggestions and activities that will enable you to meet each child's needs in very practical, effective ways.

You can use this easy-to-read book of techniques, guidelines, games and ideas as a reference for specific ways to work with individuals in a classroom. Various types of programmed materials are described, and a ready-to-use sample of a programmed booklet is included (Chapter 11). You can easily follow the complete group-language project given, which shows you how to use flexible groupings in teaching language skills, and also teaches you how to establish and maintain simple individual record-keeping. Anecdotal case studies are provided to demonstrate how enrichment projects can be handled on an individual basis over a period of time, using the small group approach.

Successful techniques are also suggested for teachers who are team teaching and for those who work in self-contained classrooms. Examples of interclass special interest group activities are given, as well as ideas for planning optional groupings in a self-contained classroom.

Games and game-like activities that can teach or give practice to individual skills are provided — activities are considered "game-like" when pupils engaged in them feel that they are playing instead of working. Game-like activities usually contain some element of chance or surprise; or they provide the excitement of planning a course of action, playing a part or solving a problem that has become the pupil's own.

You will learn how to conduct good individual conferences; and how to meet with every child according to need. Examples of good and poor conferences are given to help you get the most out of the very brief time you can spend with each pupil.

The techniques and materials presented here are all classroom-tested with a variety of primary and elementary school pupils, and were used with children who have a wide range of abilities.

Grade levels are seldom specified in this book, because children in any grade vary so much in interest and ability. Many of the activities given can be used or modified for use in more than one grade level, according to your judgment.

There is a delicate balance between individualizing enough to realize each child's potential and trying to do too much. Suggestions are given to help you achieve as much individualization as you can and should . . . comfortably and effectively. Ideas are provided that will help you avoid unnecessary repetition in cases where group lessons are by far the most efficient, productive way to motivate and teach.

Since few classroom teachers are ever able to individualize as much as they would like to, this book will also help you to relax and enjoy working with the class as a whole as well as with individuals, because of the many advantages offered by *Flexible Group Instruction.*

Rosalind Minor Ashley

ACKNOWLEDGMENTS

I am grateful for the help and suggestions given by Chuck, Steve, and Rick Ashley and Fay and Jack Minor.

And my warmest thanks to the following:

From District No. 39, Wilmette, Illinois: Dr. William J. Fritsche, Assistant Superintendent of Schools; Lisbie Goss, Marlys Washburn, Steve Pritikin, Marie Rolston, and Kenneth Scharmann, Central School; Thomas L. Berenz and Susan Huster, Howard Junior High School; Harriette Crummer, Director of Instructional Materials, and Maria Rauhauser, Instructional Materials Center.

From District No. 65 (Willard School), Evanston, Illinois: Dr. David A. Hagstrom, Principal, Donna Secrist, Librarian and Coordinator, Janice Conner, Maureen Ford, and Betty Ann Trainer.

From Sunset Ridge School District No. 29, Northfield, Illinois: Mary Osborne. Principal, Helen Mitchell, Librarian, and Peggy Pressley, Middlefork School; Martha Boos, Sunset Ridge School.

And Bradley Sussman, Northbrook, Illinois; Ruth Ann Hodnett, Clarendon Hills, Illinois; Florence Saipe, Armstrong School, Chicago, Illinois; Naperville American Association of University Women, Naperville, Illinois; Volunteer Talent Pool, Winnetka, Illinois; Volunteer Bureau of Evanston, Evanston, Illinois; Bob Thorsen's Service Station, Evanston, Illinois.

Table of Contents

1

Meeting Individual Needs
Systematically with Flexible Groupings

We need to be flexible in our groupings, using the size of group that is most effective for the task at hand. We can use large group instruction, which accomplishes many tasks well, with the necessary interaction between minds. Children with the same instructional needs can learn in small groups, with these units changing to meet their needs. Individuals will have ample opportunities for one-to-one conferences because individual conference time has not been wasted on routine matters such as general directions. Flexible grouping will give pupils the best of all methods — the excitement of a class discussion, the intimacy of small group learning and the close, individual relationship of a child alone with a teacher.

This book will show you how to be flexible as you teach, meeting the children's needs and meeting your own needs in a practical, realistic way of teaching. It will give detailed examples of flexible grouping using large groups, medium-sized groups, small groups and the teacher-child group, as required. These methods have worked well, as they harmonize our desire for accomplishment with our time and energy.

It is not a contradiction to say that you can individualize in small groups. As you do small group work each individual receives your attention and help, and you can individualize for five or six pupils at once, effectively and efficiently. Your small group can receive its directions as a unit, but each child's interaction with you can become very personal, because you have the time and proximity to be able to watch and listen for individual responses, creativity and problems.

Some children who are extremely shy because of physical or emotional problems will function better in the informality of a small teaching group.

You'll find that small groups of learners are just right for most educational games and many types of audio-visual equipment. Small groups can take turns switching from one film loop to another after each group has discussed what it has seen. Filmstrip previewers, tape recorders with headphones and many of the coordinated filmstrip and cassette lessons are ideal for small group work.

Another benefit of small group teaching is the freedom of movement that it provides for restless students — some of whom find it necessary to keep their bodies active as well as their minds.

This chapter gives tips on classroom organization and discipline and it helps you to find out what pupils' needs are and it gives an original diagnostic language test. It provides keys to planning realistic objectives and effective record-keeping. You will learn how to use audio-visual aids to individualize, how to avoid lock-step assignments, how to use pupil teachers and how to plan committee research. A small group project on studying pets is also suggested.

CLASSROOM ORGANIZATION

A classroom that is set up for flexible grouping is alive and exciting. The furniture, the learning materials and the people are ready for movement and learning activity.

Many classrooms have desks and chairs that can be moved anywhere when needed. It is especially good to have at least two small group centers that are always ready without having to move furniture, but four desks moved together can be good for a small group. One fine, informal classroom* has a large collection of big, comfortable pillows arranged right in front of the room, under the

---

*Peggy Pressley, Middlefork School, Sunset Ridge School District No. 29, Northfield, Ill.

chalkboard. When the teacher calls up a small group, they have a good place to sit and work.

Another primary teacher* provides each child with a plastic vegetable bin for storing his work and supplies. Rocking chairs, arm chairs, a small couch and rugs are comfortably available for free reading. Study carrels are provided for private work, made from large open boxes and small tables. A pile of clipboards is ready for writing when children sit on the rug away from a table.

Most rooms have one large table surrounded by chairs. This is a good place for a committee meeting, a buzz session or any other small group.

When necessary, and when desks are not needed for writing, children are very willing to sit on the floor. It works well to use all four corners of the room in order to separate working groups.

Individual conferences can be held anywhere that you have two chairs. It is often good for the teacher to sit at the back of the room for this purpose. She can keep an eye on the rest of the class, and be away from one of the symbols of her authority — the teacher's desk. This can promote relaxed rapport for conferences.

Learning centers in classrooms can be as different as the teachers who plan them. They are effective when they:

1) are changed often.
2) provide activities as well as things to look at.
3) give challenging, self-checking materials.
4) have equipment and supplies for individuals to experiment with.
5) furnish ways to record progress in independent work — charts, record sheets for listing work done etc.

You may not want to move some of your learning center materials from the table when your small groups meet, so it will be more efficient to staple them to bulletin boards, tape them on walls or use chairs and desks rather than the big table. When you need a table for experiments, you may be able to borrow an extra one for a while.

---

*Lisbie Goss, Central School, District No. 39, Wilmette, Ill.

DISCIPLINE

Classroom discipline can also vary with individual teachers and each type can be considered good although different. Some teachers can tolerate more hustle and bustle and a higher noise level than others. The main criteria to consider are whether the children are actively learning, cooperating and improving learning attitudes.

Most teachers will benefit from a re-evaluation of their discipline techniques. Ask yourself these questions:

1) Am I tired and nervous at the end of the day from too much noise?

    If so, plan more times when quiet is enforced.

2) Are some pupils taking advantage of independent activity time to visit rather than work?

    You can end this in most cases by being firm with individuals about taking away their privilege to work on their own.

3) Am I expecting the same kind of classroom discipline for all types of activities?

    If so, rethink this and make your life easier. A spelling test, a spelldown or an individualized reading period all require quiet rooms. Science experiments, committee work and some games not only generate, but cannot operate without a low hum of voices.

4) Do pupils seem irritable and distracted?

    If so, perhaps the noise and activity level is too high and pupils need more quiet times when they can concentrate.

5) Are pupils sluggish and bored?

    If so, they probably need an activity period when they can leave their desks, stretch and chat about projects with other pupils. Maybe the room is too quiet.

HOW TO FIND OUT WHAT
PUPILS' NEEDS ARE

Before you can meet a child's needs it is important that you determine what they are. This is one of the most difficult aspects of teaching, especially early in the school year before you know each child well. Some diagnostic tests, past classroom performance, past achievement test results and current observation all add up to a good beginning for grouping. You will be changing groups later as learning rates vary and new needs become apparent.

Make use of the cumulative records that are sent to you from the pupils' past teachers, as they are invaluable aids to you. Rely on the test results and comments on subject-matter achievement for some of your first groupings. However, it is wise to keep an open mind as far as comments about personality and behavior are concerned. These can be subjective opinions, and there are often differences in the way pupils interact with various teachers and classes.

Some diagnostic testing can be very useful to you early in the year; but with young children or slow readers, a verbally-oriented test may not show the true knowledge of or interest in a subject area. In these cases, oral discussion can bring out some information concerning concepts and facts.

Diagnostic testing is especially useful in mathematics and spelling. In science, working with children on experiments and talking with them about the methods and results can be more diagnostic than an objective test that measures only recall of facts. Some social studies skills can be measured by map work and testing with essay and objective questions that go beyond simple recall. But, social studies, values and attitudes can only be measured by discussion and observation of behavior in simulations and human interaction.

An example of a teacher-made diagnostic test follows: It is the pretest — post-test to be given before assigning a programmed language booklet (given in Chapter Eleven) that teaches about predicates.

This test can be used to determine whether pupils can identify:

1) a real sentence.

2) a predicate in a sentence.

PRETEST — POST-TEST

DIRECTIONS: WRITE AN X ON THE LINE BEFORE
THE ANSWER YOU CHOOSE.

1.   Choose the sentence that has the last part missing.

_____ a) The doll _____a pretty dress.

___X___ b) The doll _____ ___ _____ _____.

_____ c) _____ _____has a pretty dress.

_____ d) I don't know.

2.   Choose the real sentence from the following:

_____ a) To eat ice cream.

_____ b) Ice cream eat I like to.

___X___ c) I like to eat ice cream.

_____ d) Like to eat.

3.   In a simple sentence, a predicate tells . . .

_____ a) I don't know.

___X___ b) us something about the subject.

_____ c) us who or what the sentence is about.

_____ d) us what's in the first part of the sentence.

4.   In a simple sentence, a predicate can be found . . .

_____ a) at the beginning.

_____ b) anywhere in the sentence.

_____ c) I don't know.

___X___ d) at the end.

5.   Choose the sentence that has a missing predicate.

_____ a) _____ like to play baseball.

_____ b) I don't know.

___X___ c) Girls _____ ___ _____ _____.

_____ d) Girls _____ to play baseball.

6.   Choose the sentence which has only its predicate
underlined.

___X___ a) Many trees have green leaves.

_____ b) Many trees have <u>green leaves</u>.

_____ c) I don't know.

_____ d) <u>Many trees</u> have green leaves.

7.   Choose the sentence which has only its <u>predicate</u> underlined.

_____ a) <u>The family</u> is going on a picnic.

_____ b) The family <u>is going</u> on a picnic.

___X___ c) The family <u>is going on a picnic</u>.

_____ d) I don't know.

Figure 1-1

After the pupil completes his diagnostic pretest, mark it, keep it and let him know whether he is to do the booklet. If he answers at least six questions out of seven correctly, skip the matching booklet and go on to the next pretest. Otherwise, assign the programmed booklet.

You can construct similar multiple-choice diagnostic tests of your own. Limit them to one or two concepts and keep them simple. These tests can help you to find out if the pupil needs to study a particular concept, or if he already knows it and can go on to other work.

You will probably have written behavioral objectives for any programmed booklet that you write. Plan at least two test items for each objective. If you have too few questions on your test, a couple of lucky guesses can make the test unreliable and invalid. If you have only one or two objectives, be sure to write about three test questions for each objective.

One of the many fine diagnostic materials that can be effectively used for individualizing is DIAGNOSIS: An Instructional Aid Series-Reading. Specific objectives measured by the Probes criterion-referenced diagnostic tests, are correlated to major basal reading programs and SRA supplemental materials. Comprehension Probes in one set, Probe RA-14, cover: Fantasy and Reality, Classifying, Inferences, Facts and Details, Following Directions, Main Idea, Picture Clues, Drawing Conclusions and Sequence. There are also Vocabulary Probes, Structural Analysis Probes and many others in this set. Students work on their own with cassettes. They follow directions, complete the Probe, record any wrong answers after checking and bring the Probe to their teacher.

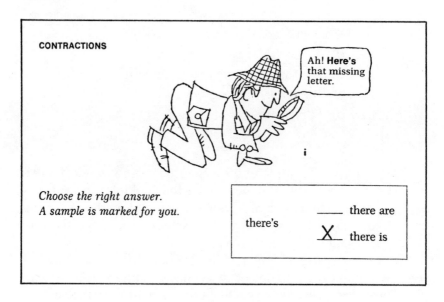

Figure 1-2*

A creative writing project can usually give you some idea of a child's language needs, as you will be able to diagnose what he needs help in by analyzing his use of sentences, spelling, punctuation and handwriting.

Creativity cannot really be measured, especially with one writing project. Because mood and inspiration are so vital to creativity, be cautious in evaluating this, and wait a long time before you make a *tentative* judgment — after many, many creative writing projects. It is difficult to know whether an idea is truly creative or imitative. However, the main need in each child is the stimulation of creativity, since creative thought enriches all learning and all life — not just writing. Encouragement and opportunities for practice will help, and these are more important than measuring creativity. All children need it.

*From DIAGNOSIS™: An Instructional Aid Series, Reading, Level A. © 1973, Science Research Associates, Inc. Used by permission of the publisher.

Music and art have many aspects, so they require specialists to determine many of a pupil's needs. But there are certain needed skills that you can pinpoint by asking a child to read notes, sing a simple melody from musical notes or use specific art materials. A child's need for information and experiences in the arts varies with his family background, home music and art training, and his individual talents and interests.

There are other needs that pupils have that are even more difficult to identify. Assume that all students have a need for recognition and success, even if they hide this. Acceptance is a universal need, as well as the need to like and respect teachers and peers. Since a need for success and acceptance is shared by all students, you can meet this by having high enough expectations to give them something to work for, with a realistic chance for success.

Some pupils need help in social relationships and cooperation, possibly because they have had few opportunities to interact well at home. Committee work or small group projects will show you those who need this special training.

A few children need extra guidance in assuming responsibility, and this can be a vital need for their growth. Daily routines and classroom tasks will show you those who need your help. With older students, homework and study hall assignments may guide you to those who cannot take responsibility.

Diagnostic testing and general discussion can be done well with an entire class. Observation and listening are done best while you work with small groups or have conferences with individuals.

Whether the child's needs are educational, personal or social, it takes time to determine them. Relax and enjoy getting to know your pupils. Talk to the children and tell them about yourself so that they can get to know you as a person with interests, likes, dislikes and needs. They will tell you all about themselves if you try to listen to them. Above all, children *need* to communicate with someone who cares.

TIPS ON PLANNING REALISTIC OBJECTIVES

First of all, be realistic about your own objectives in teaching. Many educators believe that the tutorial relationship leads to the

best learning, and they emphasize the benefits of one-to-one interaction. Although they are correct about the advantages of individualizing, they tend to forget the motivational possibilities of
group instruction. In an effort to reach an ideal, these teachers
lose the excitement and stimulation of group dynamics. As they
nervously strain for the impossible goal, they repeat the same instructions endlessly to individuals, and of course, miss some
children completely because of lack of time. In their effort to give
the best, they become tense and irritable, spending too much time
with some and ignoring others. Their ambition is laudable, but
their methods are inefficient and frustrating. So, to be realistic
you must budget your time, saving individual conferences for
when they are needed. Work with many different kinds of groups.

As far as objectives for the children are concerned, if you
concentrate on behavioral learning objectives you will be better
able to evaluate whether your students have reached them. Avoid
ambiguous terms such as *enjoy, understand* or *become familiar
with,* as they are impossible to measure. Use behavioral terms
such as *solve, answer, be able to match* or *correctly identify.* You
can observe and test such objectives.

Have high expectations, but do not be disappointed if many
of your students cannot reach them. Be generous with praise for
real accomplishments, no matter how small, and be content if
you have helped some children to make progress. Learning is not
always paced evenly. The main objective is to keep and increase
students' interest and enthusiasm for learning.

KEYS TO EFFECTIVE RECORD-KEEPING

You may still wish to keep a class grade book for entering
marks on important tests or assignments, but you will find it very
helpful to have a small notebook for each pupil in your class. It
can be ten sheets of lined paper folded vertically and stapled at
the left. Write the student's name and subject groupings on the
cover for quick reference. Have a few special pages for each
subject.

Whenever you meet with a small group or an individual,
have the appropriate notebooks handy for your reference and
so you can make notes.

When you make an individual assignment, jot it down on the correct page with the date. You then can keep track of progress as time goes by. The notebooks will tell you who needs conferences, encouragement, small group remedial work and new assignments.

If you have children using special equipment such as teaching machines, tape recorders, filmstrip previewers, programmed booklets, reading or mathematics labs or science kits, you can record their progress on the appropriate pages and insure fair distribution of equipment.

You may wish to note quickly a punctuation need, a spelling problem or a social problem as you work with or observe a child. Later on, the notebooks will serve as a reference to you when you select committees, organize pupil tutoring or plan parent conferences.

USING AUDIO-VISUAL AIDS TO INDIVIDUALIZE

There is a bewildering variety of fine audio-visual materials available, and many of them can be used independently by individuals. They can introduce a concept, reteach, practice and enrich.

Throughout this book there are suggested some teaching materials that can be useful particularly for individualizing. They represent only a few of the many fine teaching tools on the market. You will find it fascinating to look at and listen to many of them.

Search for the correct level of difficulty as well as the subject you wish to teach with them. Try to have simple practice materials as well as more difficult enrichment lessons.

When possible, skim through the booklets and listen to the records and cassettes before you use these aids. Catalogs and teachers' manuals that come with the materials also tell you a great deal about what they can teach your students.

An excellent example of an audio-visual aid is "Tayo: A Nigerian Folktale."* It is one of a series of sound filmstrip pro-

---

*"Tayo: A Nigerian Folktale," No. 300-523. Guidance Associates of Pleasantville, N.Y. 10570, a subsidiary of Harcourt Brace Jovanovich, Inc., 1971. Running time: 15 minutes.

grams for the elementary level that portray folktales and legends from various geographic areas. They are designed to stimulate discussion of cultural diversity; social origins and functions of folktales; and introductory concepts of American history.

The text on the record and the tapes have been recorded identically on both sides. One side has audible signals for use on manual equipment, and the reverse side has inaudible signals which activate the automatic advance on special combination projection units. The script text can also be used with the inaudible side manually, as it indicates each point where the filmstrip should be advanced to the next frame. The color filmstrip has seventy-six frames.

A discussion guide provides instructions, a summary of the filmstrip, suggested classroom activities, a bibliography and a complete script.

Another good elementary level sound filmstrip for social studies and guidance is "You Got Mad: Are You Glad?"* It too has a 12" banded LP record or cassette, but it has two segmented filmstrips. This lesson is about an observer to a group conflict who steps in and calms the hostile participants. Your students explore causes, effects and expressions of hostility, behavioral choices available in conflict situations and ways to resolve conflicts with minimal hostility.

Allow immediate classroom exploration of key ideas — through activities and games centered on inductive response and inquiry. The scenes for each filmstrip are photographed on location with young children of various ages, ethnic and racial backgrounds.

The first sound filmstrip, "Tayo: A Nigerian Folktale," will be useful for individual, small group or large group work. The second one mentioned is recommended for small group and full class work. For "You Got Mad: Are You Glad?"* have the entire class participate in the pre-viewing discussion. If you wish to have small groups study this while you do experiments or have conferences, it will work well to have them take turns while you are busy. Then, get together with the large group for a follow-up

---

* "You Got Mad: Are You Glad?" 2 filmstrips, 1 record, No. 320-885; 2 filmstrips, 1 cassette, No. 320-893. Guidance Associates of Pleasantville, N.Y. 10570, a subsidiary of Harcourt Brace Jovanovich, Inc.

discussion and for some of the suggested classroom activities which may be assigned on an individual basis.

AVOIDING LOCK-STEP ASSIGNMENTS

We should avoid the type of instruction that tries to teach the same thing in the same way to each child just because it seems easier. In the long run it is not, because then we must cope with the problem of having children fail. It is better to give lessons to small groups based on ability and have each child succeed in some way.

Reading, mathematics and spelling are the most important to teach in small groups, so that lessons, tests and assignments differ for children of different capacities.

Social studies, science, music and art may be taught well with large group lessons if you expect different assignments from various children. The introductory lecture, film or discussion can be valuable to all students, and there is not time enough to teach all subjects to small groups. However, reading requirements, experiments, research projects and artistic assignments must vary with individuals. Make use of pupil tutors, games, science and social studies texts written for younger pupils and simple filmstrips to practice and reteach for slower children. Encourage talented, interested students by assigning extra credit projects that you check on regularly.

HOW TO USE PUPIL TEACHERS

Some people do not realize the value of pupil tutors, and they think that if gifted students do teaching they are wasting their time. This is not true, because aside from the real *human value* of helping others, the gifted tutor gains deep insight into a subject by teaching it. He or she is required to learn much more than he teaches in order to prepare the lessons. The research alone that is necessary makes tutoring very worthwhile for the tutor. Schedule regular tutoring for individuals and small groups.

Pupil tutors will not introduce new skills, but they can be very effective in practicing and clarifying skills that have already been taught. Having just learned themselves, tutors are close to the possible learning difficulties. Many youngsters can relax more when a classmate is helping them than when their teacher does it. Sometimes a slow learner is doing all right, but will do even better with the help and stimulation of a tutor. He gains confidence and can ask repeated questions without embarrassment.

Young tutors can enrich themselves as well as those they work with by digging deeper into a unit of study, expanding it and making it seem more relevant to the interests of a slow or reluctant peer.

Another type of pupil teaching can be used to motivate bright students to outstanding effort. Every once in a while, when a report or a special project is especially well done, reward the student by telling him that his work was so good that you want him to share it with other classes. This will naturally build a resolve in the pupil to achieve further. Arrange with the other teachers in your grade level or team to have this child present his report or project to their classes.

Have a conference with the pupil well before he goes to teach the lesson. Encourage him to prepare himself to ask for and answer questions from the floor as this is an excellent way to stimulate learning in depth. Teaching well requires extensive knowledge, and the student will dig for it because he wants to be well prepared.

PLANNING COMMITTEE RESEARCH

Use capable students as chairmen of research committees. Have the entire class work in small groups to search for information in any subject.

Some of the best lessons I ever had were science research using question sheets. Each committee member had his own copy of a question sheet made up from different science textbooks.

If you are teaching third graders, guide them to their answers by specifying what book to use for each question. For older students, let them use the index and table of contents of each book in their pile to look for information on their own.

Help committee chairmen the first time you do this by showing them how to divide up the questions among their committee members. Each pupil should have three to six questions to answer, depending on his age and ability. The chairman is to do his share of the questions and then be available to help others find their answers. He is not to do the work for them, but just give suggestions and guide them to work by themselves.

When the answers are finished, have chairmen check them to make sure they are complete and in numerical order. Chairmen should read them all to see that they make sense and that they answer the questions.

Plan a separate session the same day or the following day to have the class discuss the questions and answers. Call on each chairman in turn to give his committee's answer for the particular question.

It can be fun if you wish to have the committees compete for points. I collected each group's answers after the session and marked them with points. A correct answer got one point and a very complete correct answer got one and a half points. Answers showing original thought or a great deal of research effort got as many as three points. *Individuals* were not competing — *just groups*. The next day I posted the committee scores showing the winner.

I like to use this type of lesson, because I use more than one science series, and this is a way of getting the best from each of them. It also solves the problem of having only a few books in each series. This committee work generates a lot of interest and excitement, and it is very different from usual science projects.

STUDYING PETS FOR A SMALL GROUP PROJECT

Young people of all ages love animals, and whether they have pets or yearn for them, the subject is irresistible. Begin this project for the entire class with a discussion about pets. The large group will enjoy talking about pets that have become famous in literature. You may begin with the nursery rhyme, "Mary had a little lamb" and let them take it from there.

Then move on to the topic of unusual pets and allow the class to mention a few. You may wish to give some of the following examples: In China and Japan singing crickets are kept as pets in specially designed cages; a Chinese child may have a lark. If a child lives in Mexico he may even make a pet of a flea or a cockroach. Expand pupils' interest in other countries by mentioning that the children of Australia make pets of koalas and young kangaroos.

Go on to talk about the advantages and disadvantages of keeping pets, relating them to city homes, suburban homes and farm homes. Have someone keep a list on the board showing the large variety of pets that it is possible to have.

At this point, post four or five sign-up sheets for small group reports based on research and discussion. Some possible ideas for topics may be:

Pets in Literature — Have pupils prepare a bibliography of favorite or recommended books in which the characters have pets. Children can give the title, author, publisher, publication date and a brief description of the type of story and the kind of pet in it.

Unusual Pets — The group will read and write about all kinds of wild creatures such as monkeys, raccoons and those mentioned previously which are cared for as pets. Pupils will research the special care needed, the possible dangers and the age at which some of the pets must be given up.

Advantages and Disadvantages of Keeping Pets — This group can list all of the common pets. Then they can divide into pros and cons to present the case for and against keeping animals in differing environments. This type of discussion and report can be consoling to frustrated students who are unable to keep pets because of space or care requirements.

General Care of Pets — One group may wish to study in detail how to care for various common pets. Their report will cover the animals' food, quarters, preventive shots, outdoor exercise needs and requirements for human or animal company.

After the children have been divided into small units, arrange a separate work space for each group. Provide paper, pencils and reference materials. Allow pupils to go to the library for additional books and help after they have used these references and have had their preliminary small group discussions.

Set a time when each group must begin to write its report, and announce a final time when reports are due.

You can enrich this activity by adding to your school library's resources of trade and reference books. Have ready whatever else you can find on the subject. Use magazines, encyclopedias, newspaper articles, etc.

When the group reports are turned in, allow class time for the children to share their findings in some way.

CHECKLIST

* Be flexible and use the size of group that is most efficient for the task at hand.
* Individualize effectively by working with small groups.
* Organize for small group work and one-to-one individualizing by providing comfortable furniture groupings and well-equipped learning centers.
* Re-evaluate your discipline techniques for: 1) good pupil learning and 2) pupil and teacher well-being.
* Expect pupils to behave in ways appropriate to their learning activities.
* Use some diagnostic tests, cumulative records and current observation for your beginning groupings.
* Be cautious about results of verbal tests with young children and slow readers.
* Write your own multiple-choice diagnostic tests and use professionally-made tests.
* Discuss and experiment, as well as test, in social studies and science to find out students' educational needs.
* Go deeper than simple recall in objective tests.
* Find out students' language needs by working on a creative writing project.
* Assume that each child needs stimulation and encouragement of creativity.
* Ask for help from specialists in music and art when you need it.
* Observe pupils in committees and small groups to determine their social relationships and needs.
* Watch for those who need extra guidance in assuming responsibility by assigning tasks or homework.
* Communicate with students on a human level so that they will be able to talk to you about themselves.

* Expect realistic accomplishments for yourself and your pupils.
* Avoid ambiguous instructional objectives and use behavioral objectives that you can test and observe.
* Keep individual progress notebooks for each student to record progress, needs and special equipment used.
* Use audio-visual equipment for teaching, practice and enrichment, varying the level of difficulty and the group size with the individuals.
* Try to use small groups for teaching reading, mathematics and spelling, so that lessons, tests and assignments can match the child's abilities.
* Teach social studies, science, music and art in large group lessons, but individualize assignments and projects.
* Challenge and encourage your talented students to learn more by having them teach others.
* Guide your pupil tutors by telling them what to expect and how to prepare for it.
* Use science research committees to work with question sheets and multiple texts.
* Try a small group project about pets to exploit students' natural interest in animals.

2

Teaching with Flexible Groupings in a Creative Writing Project

Use a large project to motivate children to create and work. You can plan with the entire class and then move to small group work for special tasks and extra practice sessions. Conferences with individuals can come next, so that you can try to meet each child's educational and emotional needs.

This chapter will give you simple plans for starting and carrying through one issue of a class magazine. It will begin with the initial large group motivating and idea session. The emphasis will be on helping individuals within a group environment. The class magazine will be much more than a vehicle to teach individual skills and give creative writing practice; it will also be an opportunity for the children to work and learn cooperatively. Pupils will achieve their full potential as they help others and strive for a successful group venture.

The magazine will belong entirely to the children, from the simplest task to the highest responsibility. They will be guided to plan, select a title and cover, write, proofread, edit and organize the publication.

Class assignments will be given not only according to individual talents, but also for the purpose of meeting individual needs for responsibility and leadership. Each staff and class member will grow in maturity and self-image from this experience.

Guidelines are given here for improving individual language

skills. Ready-to-use lessons are presented to help you organize pupils into special need groups for extra practice in needed skills.

Tips are given for keeping simple, individual language notebooks. You will find out how to keep easy, detailed records so that you can organize the class into small, special-need groups.

Ideas for teaching spelling, capitalization, question marks, proofreading, organization skills, handwriting, letter-writing and syllabication are presented. They will show how you can teach with flexible groupings to meet each child's needs in an efficient way.

Suggestions for inspiring creativity and effort are included. Ways are shown to exploit individual interests in the selection of topics and tasks.

The project is planned so as to encourage leadership abilities in children. It is set up so that the pupil, rather than the teacher, does the work. This, of course, will give each child a real sense of pride and accomplishment.

A CLASS MAGAZINE — AN OPPORTUNITY FOR COOPERATIVE INDIVIDUALIZED LEARNING

The beginning motivating and planning period is one of the most important. It will arouse interest in the children, and also, a desire to be a part of a group enterprise.

Some pupils, who are able to do it, will be given leadership and special work responsibilities. All of the children will learn to do their share of the work.

Have the editors' and proofreaders' names ready on the chalkboard, covered by a map, before the lesson begins. It's best not to distract the group with these names until you're ready.

Place two sheets of lined paper on each desk before class, so that you won't have to stop during the lesson. Have a popular woman's magazine ready.

Show and talk about the magazine and have the class tell you who it is written for. When someone says "mothers," tell them that your class magazine will be written for whole families — mothers, fathers and children.

Explain the duties of the editors, art editor and proofreaders, and uncover the names of the magazine staff on the board. Then, give out the special assignments that are necessary: for those with learning disabilities or other handicaps; for younger or slower pupils; and for those who need encouragement or practice in special tasks. Some of these pupils may need partners to work with, and others may need simpler assignments.

Have a brief class discussion about what a magazine like yours will include. With your help, the class will probably suggest the following, which you will write on the board, leaving plenty of space under each title for names:

Stories and Pictures   Poems   Articles

Jokes   Recipes   Ads

You can suggest a few others:

Record Review   Book Review   Letters to the Editors

TV Review   Fashions

The children will then volunteer for their choice of activity, and will take turns writing their names under the appropriate headings on the board. In cases where a child has already been given a special assignment, write his or her name under the correct heading. Allow pupils with special assignments to volunteer for another task if they wish to. However, remind all of the children who have signed up for two activities to do only one at a time, unless they are waiting for help on one.

There will probably be great interest — especially at first. If any of the children wish to take their stories or jokes home to work on, discourage them from doing this. It usually ends up with the parents doing the writing, or with the work being lost. Remind pupils not to have anyone help them when they first write their stories, and not to copy from anything. The only exception could be the measurements for a recipe. Tell children that anything they write that is their own is going to be much, much better than what they copy from someone else — because their magazine must be the children's own best work.

After the individual assignments are signed up, allow the many last minute changes that are inevitable. Many children will use this time to volunteer for an extra task.

Demonstrate with two sheets of lined paper how to make a vertical fold so that you have a small notebook with four pages. Tell the children to fold their two sheets of lined paper in the same way.

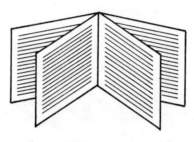

Figure 2-1

When the notebooks are folded, show how you staple them together in two places on the fold. Have each child staple his own notebook together in this way. The activity will go faster if you have at least three *filled* staplers handy in separate locations, so pupils can line up in short lines to staple their notebooks.

The children will then write their full names on the front covers, with the folds at their left. Then, they will hand their completed notebooks in to the teacher, who will keep them in alphabetical order for easy access during individual conferences.

Choosing a Title

Ask for suggestions on a title for the magazine. After title ideas are given aloud, have pupils write them on the board or take turns writing the titles on the board so that you can read them aloud. It's a good idea to read aloud everything that's put on the board, for those who may not be able to see well, and also for those who learn best by hearing.

Once the titles are on the board, give everyone a few minutes to decide on the one he wants. After that, have a vote, either with a show of hands or with written check marks after the title on the board. I prefer check marks; and I have each child come up to the board in turn, usually in groups of two to save time, to write a check mark after his favorite title. The winning title is the one with the most checks. When there is a tie between two titles, erase all the other titles and repeat the vote between the two tied titles.

We ended up with a final tie vote between *Everything for Everybody* and *Family Magazine,* so we left these two titles on the board until three absent class members could break the tie. The next day, two of the absent three voted for the first one, so *Everything for Everybody* was the winner. I liked it too.

Organizing for Individualizing

At most class meetings begin with a short session of large group instruction for all. This would include general directions that apply to everyone, and which should not be repeated to each individual. For example, remind children not to copy their work, but to use their own ideas.

Set the class to their writing assignments, and call up small groups in turn for meetings. For instance, meet with the editors and then the proofreaders to discuss and explain their respective duties again.

Meet with all of the children who are writing stories, poems and articles. This will be a medium-sized group. Offer them help by providing visual stimuli. Color pictures from magazines will prove to be very exciting to them, and most of them will take the pictures to use later. Speak about having a beginning, middle and end for a story or article.

Send part of the group back to their desks to work, and keep with you the few pupils who are writing poems. Tell them that a poem need not rhyme, and that many poems are just intense, emotional or beautiful language. Some of these children may want to use the pictures too.

Then, call up those who are working on jokes. Some of these children need help in getting started too, so show them the remaining pictures. Remind these pupils again not to copy jokes, but to make up their own or write old jokes in their own words, if possible.

Last of all, conduct a few individual conferences with those who signed up on the four conference sign-up sheets posted in different locations in the room. Try to remember to take first those who placed X's before their names to signify urgency.

Tell editors to help pupils with their work — with spelling, punctuation and with using the dictionary — encouraging as much as correcting. Allow children to help each other, go to editors or team up on projects if they wish to. Emphasize that they are to work together, not copy from each other. Proofreaders will help each other, and they will also assist those whose papers they check.

If you have any children who are unable to write because of some handicap, have them dictate their story or poem into a tape recorder (or to you or a friend). Then, when the story is written and O.K.'d by proofreaders and editors, allow some child of low ability (who has good handwriting) to copy the story on the ditto-master for the handicapped child.

Near the end of the project you will find that some children have made four or five contributions, and others only part of one. Encourage those who have been successful and prolific to complete what they're working on and then work to help the slow ones finish their stories or jokes.

MATCHING ASSIGNMENTS TO INDIVIDUAL ABILITIES

Get to know your children's abilities before you give them as-signments. Write the word *Editors* on the board, and under it have the names of about four capable boys and girls. Select two who are able to run the magazine, and two who will benefit from learning how to accept responsibility.

Choose an Art Editor — someone who has talent or interest (or both) in art. It also should be one who will gain from being responsible for a project.

Ask a few students who like to draw to be responsible for one fashion page each. Explain that a fashion page will include draw-ings and paragraphs describing the fashions.

GUIDELINES FOR IMPROVING INDIVIDUAL LANGUAGE SKILLS

Plan to have individual conferences after all large and small group lessons, as time permits. To insure fairness, tell pupils to use the sign-up sheets when they want to see you. Try to see their work before they turn it in to editors. If you can't get to it, then check it before a dittomaster is issued to them from the editor after proofreading.

Encourage pupils to write X before their names on the list if they need urgent help and cannot go on without it. If you're busy and children need spelling help, tell them to skip a word and go on with their stories. if they can. If not, while waiting for a conference, they could draw a cover picture or read a book.

Spelling and Dictionary Skills

Use a system of Dictionary Helpers to avoid conference congestion due to individuals needing help with spelling words. Select three or four capable children who do well at spelling and at using dictionaries. Keep their names on the board, and tell the group to consult with these Dictionary Helpers or with the editors when they need help in spelling a word.

Ask these helpers not to find the words for pupils, but to help them find the words by themselves, as you do. Announce to the whole group that the helpers will not do their work for them. Say that they will help by giving beginning letters and by working with pupils as they use dictionary guide words to find the words for themselves.

During an individual conference, one child was complaining that he couldn't find the word *wanted* in the dictionary. I waited as he slowly found the correct dictionary page and shook his head because *wanted* wasn't listed.

"How about *want?*" I asked. "It's there."

His little finger pointed to the entry and he shook his head again.

"Read what it says after *want*. I'll bet you've got it," I suggested.

He read further and found the word *wanted* listed at the end of the entry for *want*.

"Good. You found it. You see, sometimes you can find the word in the dictionary if you take off the endings like *s, ing* or *ed*. Then you'll find the word you want right near the shorter one."

He was very relieved as he copied the spelling for his word.

This child was a second grader, but this same method is used to help third graders in the class. Of course, guide words are to be used by children of all ages.

Watch for spelling errors during individual conferences. If they have not been circled and corrected yet by proofreaders or editors, circle the words and copy them in the individuals' language notebooks for later practice and testing.

Then, enter all new words in each child's spelling notebook.

These words will be practiced with his other individual words during the regular spelling time.

Capitalization

Check the individual notebooks for notes on children who have problems with capital letters. Call these pupils up for a small group oral lesson at the board.

You may wish to write your own paragraph that relates to other class activities. The following may also be used for this purpose:

simple macHines

the Children are studying simple machines. they are learning about inclined planes, levers, screws, Pulleys, wedges and wheels and axles. mary and nancy did an Experiment on pulleys. they did a Good job on it.

Begin the lesson by saying, "Well — it looks as if we have a lot of work to do to fix this up. I see so *many* mistakes!"

By then, hands will be waving as the children vie with each other to be called on. If someone wants to change something that is really correct, thank him with a smile and ask him to try again.

Question Marks

Have a small group meeting of all the children who need special work on question marks. Later in this chapter you'll read how to keep simple records so that you can quickly jot down a list of children who need this meeting.

The following paragraph can be ready on the board or over-head projector: (Call it a lesson and don't mention question marks.)

Why

Why are we having this lesson. It is not to teach us about periods. Do you think it is about commas. Can you guess what this special lesson is about.

To announce the special meeting, call off the necessary names and invite anyone else who is interested to join you. When the children are ready at the board, read this paragraph aloud with its important inflections, starting with the title. Then ask the group if there are any things missing in the paragraph. Tell them that it looks incorrect to you. By then hands will be in the air.

One child told me that the punctuation was wrong, but he couldn't tell me what it was. Then, one by one, we gradually corrected the errors in the paragraph. When the group thought they were through, I noticed that they had missed one question mark. I read the question aloud with the raised inflection at the end. The children gleefully corrected it, and I praised them for a job well done. I read the paragraph again, pointing out the one sentence that was not a question, and that it correctly had a period.

I asked, "What kind of lesson was this?"

They answered, "On question marks!"

Proofreading (Checking Spelling, Punctuation, Capitalization, Paragraphing etc.)

As soon as all the children have made a start on their individual projects, plan a large group proofreading lesson to open the work period. This can be done on the chalkboard with two colors of chalk, but it is even more effective when an overhead projector is used.

We began our lesson with the following story projected on a screen in black, written with a special visual aid pen:* (I composed the story rather than embarrass a child by using his.)

april 29, 19--

birds

I like to lok at birds In the springtim They are
Prette Wy do Birds fli south in wenter Do you kno wy
       robins is one uf mi favorit bird, Dont furget the
eagl, Thats a bird to I saw a very large and prett
y bird saturday

Before class I checked to make sure that the manuscript writing on the transparency was clear and dark. I had tried not to handle the plastic sheet too much, as it is possible to have places where the ink doesn't take because of oil from your fingers.

---

*Vis-a-Vis Visual Aid Pens for Overhead Projector Transparencies. (No. K-16) black, red, blue, green. Sanford's, Bellwood, Ill.

The children giggled as they looked at the story before I read it aloud. "I have a story here that needs some proofreading. Will you help me to correct it?"

Many hands were up.

As the children directed me, I made the more obvious corrections, using a pen with red ink. Some of the capitalization was corrected:

A

ǿpril 29, 19--

B

ǿirds

We corrected spelling by circling the misspelled words and writing the correct words in the margin.

An i was dotted in red, and indentation was shown to be missing with a symbol:

We went on to add missing periods in red ink. Then we talked about capital letters and where they belonged — on names, titles, at the start of sentences. Soon more hands were in the air, and we took out the capital letters that didn't belong on words in the middle of sentences:

i

Ⱥn

When I saw no more hands in the air, I asked, "Do you see anything missing at the ends of sentences — or do you see the incorrect thing there?"

That started a wave of corrections on question marks and periods. One boy discovered the comma that should have been a period.

No one noticed the missing apostrophe in the contractions, so I wrote the following words separately on a blank space at the bottom of the sheet:

do not

that is

"How do we write these so they will say 'don't' and 'that's'?" I asked.

One child suggested taking out the *o* in *not* and the *i* in *is*.

dont
thats

"Thank you. Does that look correct?"

Everyone nodded that it did. I stood there smiling. "Are you sure? Isn't something missing?"

They were perplexed. I went on. "Isn't something missing to show that we took out a letter?"

"Oh! Oh! A dot!" someone shouted.

"Yes. You got it. It looks like a dot or a comma. It's called an *apostrophe*. Remember our lesson on apostrophes?"

Now everyone nodded that he remembered.

I wrote in a large apostrophe in red in each contraction:

don't
that's

We went back to the proofreading story, and then the contractions were quickly corrected for apostrophes. The *is* was changed to *are*, and *bird* to *birds*. The second *pretty* was divided between the two *t's*, and the rest of the capitals were fixed.

After the large group lesson, meet with your special proofreaders and repeat your instructions to them. Refer to the group proofreading lesson as an example of how pupils are to check and correct each story. Ask for questions, and help them whenever you can.

It may seem that you're not individualizing when you have the large and small group sessions, but it would be wasteful to repeat vital lessons like these for each child, when they *all* need them badly. Later, when working individually, you can refer back to the story you all corrected, and it will be more effective when you work on a single child's weak spots.

When you next have individual conferences, continue with proofreading. Check individual weaknesses, and have each child tell you how to correct his own paper.

Organization Skills

Emphasize planning and organization in all of the magazine's activities. Just as you taught organization in the stories and articles — to have a beginning, a middle and an end — do this in the planning of the magazine as a whole.

As you approach the end of your project, work with your editors to organize the magazine into a logical, planned sequence. Have them check through the final dittomasters and correct the worst errors. Some, like handwriting and paragraphing errors, are unavoidable and should be ignored. After the final checking, the editors will organize the magazine into parts. Suggest that they probably will want the letters to the editors first, the fashions together, the recipes together, and stories, ads, poems, jokes and reviews scattered throughout the magazine.

When the editors are satisfied with the magazine's plan, they will then number the dittomaster pages so that the numerals will not be too near the edge and be lost. After that, they will list the magazine's contents on a special Table of Contents page that will follow the cover picture.

The Table of Contents will list the title or type of written material, the author or artist's name and the number of the page where it will be found, in page order. The editors will probably decide to list the ads with proper credits too, even though an ordinary magazine excludes name and page credits for these. There may be two or three pages in the Table of Contents.

A typical Table of Contents could start as follows:

TABLE OF CONTENTS

		Page
Letters to the Editors .... Jane Ling,		
Bobby Erinson and Martha Brown		1
Ad .... Susie Hanson		2
Record Review .... Tom Henderson		3
Jokes .... Judy Hanover, John Mantoni,		
Rita Cannon and Robert Day		4
Story .... Elsie Miller		5
Poem .... Cindy Hutchins		6

Handwriting

Give generous praise for good handwriting, and have frequent drills on weaknesses in special letters. Use every chance for extra practice.

It seemed a wonderful opportunity when the one blind child in our class needed someone to copy her story on a dittomaster. I chose a slow child whose main skill is good, clear handwriting. By choosing him for this special assignment and telling him it was because of his good manuscript writing, I was able to get a necessary job done, and at the same time build up a slow child's self-confidence.

Letter-writing

You may want to begin one workshop with a brief, large group lesson on letter-writing. Have the following (or something similar) on the chalkboard as a model:

> 779 Elm St.
> Glenview, Illinois 60025
> May 2, 19--

Dear Editors,
    I would like to see some dog stories in your magazine. Thank you.

> Your reader,
>
> John Smith

Read the letter aloud and call attention to the capitals, indentation, heading, salutation or greeting and closing.

Discuss possible reasons why someone would write a letter to a magazine editor, and suggest praise, criticism and suggestions if they are not mentioned. In your case, with no previous magazine issues, suggestions would be the most logical reasons for letters.

Tell the class that those who have the time may wish to write a letter to the magazine editors. It will give them good practice in letter-writing. Follow this up a few days later with a large group dittomaster letter lesson.*

---

*Peggy Pressley, Middlefork School, Sunset Ridge School District No. 29, Northfield, Ill.

HEADING   *66 Maple Street*
                 Alpine, Michigan 42641
                 May 17, 19--

GREETING *Dear Jean,*

BODY   *I will be coming to your hometown. I'd like to visit you when I am there. Will you be free on Saturday, May 26? I will call you later to check this out.*

CLOSING   *Your friend,*

SIGNATURE   *Betsy*

Betsy Rogers
66 Maple Street
Alpine, Michigan 42641

ENVELOPE   *Miss Jean Harris*
                1700 Forest Drive
                Fenwick Park, California 94026

Figure 2-2

Syllabication

For second graders, this need not be taught. When third graders make errors in dividing words, make corrections for them with no emphasis on it. In my opinion, there are too many other things they need to concentrate on more at this time.

When you see double letters divided incorrectly as you have individual story conferences, point out the word and ask the child if he'd like to divide it in another place. If he doesn't know how to correct the syllabication, remind him of the group proofreading lesson and how the class divided the word correctly:

pret-ty

Then, commend the child when he makes the correction.

Oral Reading

Since there is so little time in a school day to do all the other necessary things, oral reading does not get the time it should. Use individual conference times as opportunities to hear pupils read aloud.

There will be extra benefits from this, aside from the vital oral reading practice. In some cases it will save you from embarrassing the child by telling him that you can't read or understand his story. The pupil will read it aloud to you and fill in words that may be missing that could keep you from understanding it. Secondly, this is the best way to get the child to proofread. In many, many cases, the errors we all work so hard to correct on writing projects can be found by the author himself if he would only *read* his own work. As you sit and listen appreciatively, the child will grab his pencil and add words, periods and capitals. He may catch his own spelling and handwriting errors, too. It's much better when he finds his own.

It's a good idea to begin one work session with a reminder to pupils to read through their stories or jokes before they hand them in or come up for a conference. Suggest that they look for their own corrections in the way the class did in their proofreading lessons. Tell them that they'll be reading their stories aloud to you in conferences, and it will help if they read them through ahead of time.

TIPS FOR KEEPING SIMPLE INDIVIDUAL RECORDS

There is one main reason for keeping individual records for children, and that is: you can help them to learn what they need to know and not waste time and energy on teaching them what they do not need. Since the records are for you alone, any method that works for you will be good.

Some simple types of individual notebook entries will be given here as examples of easy record-keeping. As you work with your own pupils, you will probably devise different, and better, ways of keeping notes. The less that you write the better, as your time with each child is short, and you don't want to waste it. Also, you cannot remember individual needs and skills after ten or twelve conferences in a language session, so it's best not to wait to make your entries.

The posted conference lists make it easy for you to give turns fairly. Each child who finishes a conference crosses out his name on the list and tells you whose name is next. Because the record notebooks are piled in alphabetical order, it is easy to find the child's book as he walks to your desk for a conference.

While the pupil greets you, you have time to enter the date. As you work with him, enter short notes, using the time that the child takes for making corrections, answering your questions and going up to the list to give you the name of the next pupil to come up.

Some typical notebook pages for different individuals are given here. Parenthetical explanations are not written, as the symbols and abbreviations take their place. Words are for spelling list.

4/17 — (story)

> ? ¶ (needs work with indenting and question marks)

> was
> answer

- -

4/17 — (poem)

> exc. man. (for excellent manuscript)
> cr. (for creative)

> were

- -

4/17 — ˇ(article)

> punct. (needs punctuation work)
> dict. (needs dictionary skills)

> wanted
> hear

- -

4/17 — (joke)

> syll. (needs syllabication help)

> fine
> lady

- -

4/17 — (story)

    caps (needs capitalization work)
    better   • (needs work with periods)

Use these notebooks as an easy way to keep your own records. By making quick notations, you can keep up with the amount of work each pupil is doing. Later, you will have a record of the new spelling words for pupils' individual lists.

At the first conference, make a note of what project a child is working on. For example: poem, article, joke, story etc.

When the writing is finished and being proofread, circle the word as a signal that the work is done, but not checked and copied on a dittomaster. For example: (poem)

After the checking process, and after the poem is copied on a dittomaster, place a check mark before the circled word to tell yourself that the project is completed. For example: ✓ (poem)

By making a quick check through the notebooks, you can be aware of the children who are not doing the minimum amount of work you expect for them. Be sure to schedule conferences with them as soon as you can. They are just as high a priority as those with X's before their names on the conference lists. You'll soon find out that some children request more conferences than others, and in fact, some sign up for more than they need. The child who does not ever sign up may be in the most trouble of all, so watch for this one.

CREATIVITY CATALYSTS

For our large group lesson the following was ready on the chalkboard:

ARTICLES

hobbies
how to make something
trips
current events
an interesting person

STORIES
<u></u>

	Realistic	Fantastic
	something that happened to you	fairies
	something that could have happened to you	ghosts
	family	talking animals
	western	science fiction
	sports	
	mystery	

POEMS
<u></u>

that rhyme	ABOUT:	something beautiful
		a feeling
that do not rhyme		something funny
		a story

As I read everything aloud, I lingered on the ideas for stories. When I mentioned mystery stories I asked the class what kind of characters they might have in a mystery story. Hands flew up, and one child said, "A detective."

"Yes. Good," I answered, "and in your story a child or another member of the family could be a kind of detective trying to solve the mystery. What else does a mystery have in it besides a detective of some kind?"

"Something missing," one answered.

"Yes," I said. "It could be something like *The Case of the Missing Spectacles.*"

I called on another child who suggested, "Someone killed."

"Yes. Either one would be in a mystery. What else would you have to have in your story so that the detective could find the thing that's missing?" (I was trying to take the emphasis off the idea of killing someone.)

The hands were waving. "Clues!" someone said.

I explained the word in case they were not all sophisticates. "Good. And we know that a clue is something we put in the story so that the reader and the detective will be able to solve the mystery. Do you think a mystery story is easy to write?"

They all shook their heads negatively.

"Correct. It's not easy, but some of you might want to try one. You can only do it if you plan it ahead. Don't worry about it. Just plan it and write it, and I'm sure it'll be fine."

Then we began individual conferences, and I spoke to a boy who was at a loss for a story idea. In the past he had only been able to write about one sentence in a story, so he had been assigned a joke. The short joke was written, and now he wanted to write a story for the magazine.

"What kind of a story would you like to write?" I asked.

"I don't know."

"Look up there." I pointed to the suggestions on the board. "Is there anything there that appeals to you?"

After a few minutes of hard thought, he announced, "I'm going to write a mystery story."

I didn't discourage him by telling him it was too hard for him. He was smiling broadly when he left me.

A few minutes later, he interrupted a conference to wave his paper in my face. The title of his story was *The Mistery of the Missing Spektikls.*

"I started my mystery," he gloated.

"Great. I'm looking forward to seeing it. Remember to put in some clues. Now, work on it until it's your turn for a conference."

A very short time later he was back with the first paragraph. That, with the title, was more than he had written all year. It still wasn't his turn for a conference, so I glanced at it briefly with my arm on his back.

"It looks good. Be sure to plan the ending, and have a few clues for your detective."

"I will," he reassured me with a grin.

(I allow some small interruptions from those who aren't signed up, when it seems *urgent.*) Then I went back to my conference, trying to solve the mystery of why a mystery story got him so fired up.

One afternoon, after a field trip, we began work on our magazine, and everyone was busy writing. I started individual conferences with a girl who had put a large X before her name on the conference sheet.

"I already wrote a recipe, but now I want to do a story."

"Good."

"But, I can't think of anything," she complained.

I was ready for her. "How about writing about our field trip this morning?"

She looked doubtful, but she didn't say no.

"I'm sure that all the parents who read the magazine would like to know about what we saw at the museum," I said.

"O.K." she answered, satisfied.

Use pictures from magazines, newspapers, ads etc., and show them to children to spark story, poetry or article ideas. I had very good results with the following types of pictures:

> people tobogganing with a parachute
> a butterfly chrysalis on a branch
> a large fish measuring a fisherman with a tape measure
> Hawaiian girls in traditional costumes
> a man golfing
> a hammer and a broken piggy bank
> a cowboy with a herd of horses
> a couple running on a beach
> a motorcycle
> a gorilla looking out of his cage at people
> Napoleon in his court, honoring a soldier
> an elegantly dressed lady at a dinner table with a large
>   leopard
> a mother holding a crying baby
> a boy and a girl riding horses
> a girl walking and holding hands with a large bear
> a man at a party, reaching into a fishbowl for a goldfish
> a man shooting a gun at his car
> people skiing
> a rabbit family dressed in human clothes
> two prizefighters fighting
> a man riding a bicycle
> a boy sitting beside a pup tent in the desert
> a woman playing an organ
> an ocean liner

> a man wearing an electric plug for a hat, surrounded by TV
> sets, coffee pots, irons and electric tools

I held a small group meeting with the pupils who needed ideas for stories. We discussed each picture, and we laughed over some of them. The children were grabbing pictures long before I offered them, and luckily, there were no conflicts. If there had been, the one whose last name comes first in the alphabet would have won the picture. Naturally, we wouldn't want to duplicate a story in one magazine issue by using the same picture twice. However, if that is the only way to spark a story for both children, I'd allow it, having them take turns with the picture. Their stories would probably be completely different anyhow.

EXPLOITING INDIVIDUAL INTERESTS

One girl in my class drew well and loved art work. I asked her if she would like to do a fashion page with drawings of women and girls wearing beautiful clothes with written descriptions of the fashions. She was very enthused about it. Then, another girl asked if she could do a fashion page too. Of course, I allowed it, as the interest and desire is much more important than the child's drawing ability.

A pupil signed up for a conference to wistfully tell me that he couldn't think of anything to write an article about. I asked him what he liked to do after school, and he answered, "Play, and read."

So, I suggested that he might want to write about a book he liked. He nodded negatively. Then, I asked him if he liked to play baseball when he went out to play.

He answered yes to that, so I mentioned that he could write an article about what a first baseman or a pitcher does in a game. Usually that would get someone going, but I was still batting zero.

Then I suggested that he look through the magazine pictures for an idea. He sighed and said he'd already done that.

I pointed to the ideas that I had put on the board for our large group lesson, and I read them aloud again. We went over them one by one to see what interested him. His eyes lighted up a little when I reread "science fiction," so I pursued it further. "In science fiction you can write about any kind of planet or people you like. Just

make up anything you want to about people or places out in space."
He nodded and smiled and ran to his desk to write.

ENCOURAGING LEADERSHIP ABILITIES

At the very start, as the pupils volunteer for or are assigned types of writing, the four editors copy the assignment lists from the board. As the children sign up on the board under the appropriate headings, each editor copies the list for future reference.

Tell the art editor about his responsibilities. All art work will be handed in to him or her, to be kept in a special folder. The art editor is to help, encourage and make suggestions on all illustrations. He or she is also responsible to select a cover picture from all those that are submitted. After all the illustrations are ready, the art editor gives them to the other editors, including the cover picture that was chosen.

Have a meeting with your four editors to discuss their duties, and to answer any questions they may have, as they usually worry a bit about the procedures at the start. Patiently repeat to them about keeping their records, helping authors with their stories and passing all work on to the proofreaders. Then, remind them to circle a child's name when the work is first turned in, and to check each circled name ($\checkmark$) when the work is completed. Wait until later to have a discussion about the dittomasters. Make sure that these beginning procedures are understood first.

Meet with the proofreaders to help them understand their duties. A good way to help them is to use a dark colored pencil on one of the papers, showing them how to mark a paper without crossing out or covering up any of the writing. Suggest or demonstrate the following:

1. Circle all misspelled words, and draw a line to the correctly spelled word in the margin. Encourage proofreaders to look up doubtful spellings. In case proofreaders are too busy, have them bring the paper to author and have author look up spelling with one of the Dictionary Helpers.

2. Correct for capitals at start of each sentence and on names and titles.

3. Correct for punctuation — periods, question marks, exclamation marks and apostrophes.
4. Check for titles and authors' full names.
5. Check to see if sentences make sense.
6. Suggest paragraphs when needed.
7. Suggest endings if they seem to be missing.

One proofreader made an excellent suggestion of a procedure that I hadn't thought of. She said, "I'm going to give my papers to the other two proofreaders when I'm done with them, so they can catch the mistakes I didn't get." I thought that was a wonderful idea, and from then on, the three proofreaders traded papers and did fine jobs on them. Some of my best ideas have come from my pupils!

PLANNING THE WORK SO THAT THE PUPILS DO IT

Tell children at the beginning that this will be their magazine, not yours. So — they must do all of the work, with your help. Explain the procedure:

1. They write a story, poem, article, joke, recipe, letter, ad or review, and put their full name on it.
2. Halfway through, or when needed, they sign up for a conference with the teacher. They sign up with an X in front of their names if they're having urgent problems.
3. After receiving help or comments from the teacher, they make any changes in writing, if needed. They copy it over only when it is very hard for them to read.
4. They hand in the writing to one of the editors, who circles their name to show that the work is in.
5. All illustrations for stories, fashions, recipes or ads, and suggested cover ideas, are to be turned in to art editor.

6. Editors read the work and make necessary suggestions for changes, which are then done.

7. When work is finally in with corrections, editors turn it over to proofreaders for checking.

8. Proofreaders make necessary changes with colored pencils and return work to authors. They have conferences with authors about changes when necessary.

9. Authors turn in corrected work to editors, who place check marks (✔) before the pupils' names. Editors see that this is done on the other three editors' lists.

10. When editors are satisfied with the work, they give dittomasters to authors so they can neatly copy their stories. They remind them to take out middle brown sheets before they start. Some stories or articles will end in the middle of a page, so the editors will try to see that something else is copied to fill out the dittomaster page. Short jokes or ads are suitable for this. Extra capable people will help with some of the copying.

11. The editors decide on the order of the written material in the magazine.

12. The pages are numbered.

13. The editors prepare a Table of Contents, with authors' names and page numbers.

14. The editors will assemble and staple the magazine, with the teacher's help in stapling, after she runs it off.

It is best to give a brief overview of this procedure at the start, and wait to get down to details as the work progresses. For example, there is no need to teach how to copy stories on dittomasters until the first few pupils are ready to do it.

At that time, start the class with a large group session on how to use a dittomaster. Demonstrate the dittomaster and explain its parts:

1. the white page that is written on

2. the brown protector sheet that must be taken out while writing, and put back later to prevent smudging

3. the black carbon paper

Draw a rectangle on the board as you make the following suggestion: "Leave a large margin or edge of at least one inch all around the page as you write." Then show the margin visually.

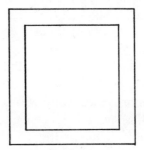

Figure 2-3

This will help to prevent the loss of some words and page numerals near the edges as the dittomasters are run off. If children forget to leave the margins, accept the work anyway — and try to adjust the dittomasters by folding them or reversing them when you run them off.

Have someone tell the class why it is so important to be careful in writing on the dittomaster. One girl told them, "You can't erase!"

Explain the procedure of scraping off errors with a razor blade that only the teacher is allowed to use. Tell the class that you don't mind scraping off errors, and not to be upset when they make them, since everyone makes mistakes. Say that the reason why you want pupils to be extra careful is that you don't want to spend too much of their conference time on scraping errors — that you'd rather be helping them with other things.

Up to the point where you must scrape errors off the dittomasters, the children have done all the work. Of course, the final stage of running off the dittomasters must be done by you. However, you can see to it that it is a fast, satisfying process if you have the pupils follow these directions about preparing the dittomasters. They will have to be repeated for emphasis:

1. Allow generous margins *all* the way around.

2. Press down while writing so that all the writing will print.

3. Place page numerals and names well inside the margin — not on the edge.
4. Have teacher make corrections on the dittomaster with tape or a razor blade. Never cross out.

All problems in running off dittomasters come from not following these directions. It takes a great deal of time to have editors go over writing that is too faint to see. The corrections must be made once on the master — not on thirty or so magazine pages.

Each editor should have a stack of dittomasters to give to pupils after the stories are O.K'd by them and by the proofreaders.

As the project approaches completion, start the group lesson by announcing that those people who have three or more stories or articles written should complete them on dittomasters and not write any more at this time. They are to finish up and then begin to help others in any way they can. This will make the proportion of stories by each pupil more fair. It will also help to wind up the project, since some children can keep writing story after story. In this way, the prolific ones will be stopped for this issue, and they will be available to help those who have difficulty getting even a few sentences together.

Be sure to have the pupils make the major effort on this magazine in order for them to get the most benefit from its production. One day, as I looked at the pile of individual notebooks to be checked, the pile of completed dittomasters with errors in them and the long list of people signed up for conferences, I began to be overwhelmed by all that I had to do. Then, I noticed the editors scurrying around the room with their lists, checking on contributions. I laughed to myself and began to relax and enjoy the magazine again. I knew it was in good hands, and that somehow, in some form, it would get done, and it would be *their own*.

The Final Stages

Have an editors' meeting to check over the final dittomasters and suggest necessary changes on them. At the same time, try to work with the one or two slow pupils who need help to finish up. In case you're too busy at this point with scraping off errors, assign one of the editors to assist the slow child in using the dictionary and in checking the work for final copying.

Wind up the work on the magazine by announcing the date you're going to begin publishing. Urge those whose work isn't in yet to finish as soon as possible.

Organize a few periods so the group as a whole will be busy with other written material and use this time to work with the editors and the few slow ones who need help.

Show the editors how to set up the magazine with stories, jokes, poems and ads scattered throughout. They will probably want to keep the recipes and fashions together, if possible. However, if some come in late, scatter them and don't worry about it.

Have some of the editors check the dittomasters for errors, and help a few others to write the Table of Contents as they number the pages. It is very important to give full credit for all contributions, so see that the editors check for this.

Accept last-minute offerings until publication time. Save the last page of the Table of Contents for the end. In this way, you can add new contributions until the final minute.

You will be pleasantly surprised to see how many errors the editors will catch in a relaxed atmosphere. Keep the razor blade handy for corrections as the editors scan the final pages and want to make changes or correct errors. Do it good-naturedly, as this work should not be full of stress, but a time of rapport with fellow workers.

Have editors check the incomplete Table of Contents against their records, and cross off each child's name. In this way, you can be sure that every pupil has work of some kind in the magazine. The editors are responsible for reminding and keeping after those few whose work is not in.

Before you run off the masters, examine each one to make sure that page numerals and every letter show up on the inked side.

If the writing is too close to the top or the bottom of the page, reverse the master as you run it off and you won't lose any of the writing. In case you have written material too close to the edge, it is sometimes easier to scrape off the numeral or name near the edge and then write it further in.

Editors can write these corrections, as well as go over faint writing on masters that won't show up in printing. After the pages are run off, they must check for wrinkled or blank pages which should be discarded.

Always run off one single copy as a test before you run off the thirty copies. Then you can change the master or its position, if necessary. While running off the magazine, if material is too close to one side you can usually move the master over or fold under a part so that you don't lose the writing. In case you spot a missing letter or numeral on the test sheet, it is much easier to write it in on the master once than to repeat it thirty times. This check will save a great deal of time and effort.

If your magazine has many pages, do the running off in two or three short sessions. Otherwise, you will get tired and be less inclined to make the few corrections on the masters that will be needed. Use paper clips to separate finished pages in stacks.

It is very exciting to assemble the magazine, and it will disrupt the class if you try to do it during school hours. Try to schedule it for recess time or after school.

Then, when all the pages are ready to assemble, have the editors lay the stacks on a table in numerical order following the cover and Table of Contents pages. As the editors put the magazine together, they will clip the pages to make magazine copies. When the thirty or so copies are assembled, have the editors check each copy to make sure the pages are in correct order.

The very final stage is stapling the magazine together in the left hand corner, not too near the edge so it might tear, and not too far in so material will be hidden. Demonstrate on the first copy. The work will go fast if you have a filled stapler for each editor. If the magazine is very thick, you may have to do the stapling, repeating the process from the front and the back.

In case the editors find some errors during assembling, correct those that you have time to do, and disregard the rest. Place emphasis on the pride pupils feel in the class accomplishment, and not on perfection.

As you pass out the completed copies, praise all the children for working so hard on their magazine. But, most important of all, be understanding about the limitations of your contributors and staff, especially if they are very young. The proofreaders will miss most of the errors, and the editors will too; besides that, the editors will not be able to keep good records on work assignments or know where the work is. In fact, one of my editors lost his own story, then wrote a poem, and lost that too!

The entire class will be very proud of its publication. This will be because it contains their written work, and because *they* worked so hard to publish it.

CHECKLIST

* Organize all teaching into large group, medium-size group, small group and individual work sessions according to special needs.
* Begin your motivating session by showing and discussing a magazine.
* Explain the duties of all staff members and give special assignments.
* Allow pupils to volunteer for the kind and amount of writing they wish to do.
* Show children how to make individual notebooks for your use in recording their needs and progress.
* Supervise a class vote on the magazine's title.
* Provide visual stimuli and organization instruction for those who are writing stories, poems and articles.
* Give special instruction to those who are writing poems, stressing the importance of intense, emotional or beautiful language rather than rhyming.
* Meet with pupils who are writing jokes, to help them get started on original jokes, or to use their own words for familiar ones.
* Conduct individual conferences with those who sign up, and give priority to those who mark their names with X's.
* See those pupils who do not sign up for conferences, as they need you most of all.
* Place emphasis on pupils helping each other with their work.
* Select some editors for their need of responsibility, as well as some for their ability.
* Use individual conferences, small group meetings and entire class sessions for improving individual language skills.
* Keep individual records as simple as you can, writing short notes, symbols and spelling words for future use.
* Use chalkboard suggestions about mystery stories, science fiction stories etc. for sparking creativity.
* Try visual stimuli, field trips and personal interests as creativity catalysts.

* Encourage leadership abilities by supervising editors as *they* do the work.
* Teach proofreaders their duties so that they can help others.
* Plan the work of the magazine so that everyone understands the procedure, giving details as needed.
* Give special instruction to all on using dittomasters to prevent later publishing difficulties.
* Stop prolific pupils after three or so contributions and have them help slow ones, to balance the amount of work in the magazine by each child.
* Do final publishing and assembling in stages in order to have high quality work and a relaxed staff.
* Make final changes once on the master rather than doing it after all the pages have been run off.
* Allow for the limitations in ability of your staff and contributors.
* Place emphasis, not on perfection, but on the children's pride in their class accomplishment.

3

Teaching Individuals and Small Groups in a Self-Contained Classroom

The self-contained classroom is still the most common kind of teaching arrangement. We must work within its limitations, but it can be a delightful way to teach and learn. For example, with a small class, or with a student teacher or a teacher aide, the self-contained classroom has many advantages such as rapport between pupils and teacher and detailed knowledge and understanding of each child by the teacher. In such cases, small group work and individualizing can work out well.

However, with a large class and no other person in the room, the demands are too great on a teacher. Much less small group work and individualizing can be done because of the greater number of students and distractions.

The idea of flexible groupings is that the size of the group varies with the activity or the concept or skill that is being taught. So, in any subject, you can group and regroup as needed — thus eliminating some of the stigma that can possibly be attached to rigid ability groupings. If a child is called up to work with you in several different groups for various types of practice he will not be able to label himself as slow or brilliant — either of which could cause him harm.

The individual conference is something that must be achieved once in a while for each child in your class. No matter how large your group may be, it is important to a child's ego that you devote some time to him alone. Chapter Seven, "Teaching with Individual Conferences," will cover this in detail.

This chapter will discuss how to use small groups to teach individuals, it will give a practical way to individualize science experiences and an interesting science demonstration. It will provide some keys to achieving group goals and give some suggestions on motivating with freedom. It includes some interesting individual learning activities, specific ways to let the community teach and some examples of effective individualized learning.

HOW TO USE SMALL GROUPS
TO TEACH INDIVIDUALS

I question the use of the usual three reading groups. Four or five, or more, which meet for different purposes with varying members, could be much more effective. With smaller groups you could interact better with individuals and find out their specific reading needs, and it would be easier for you to keep a good notebook on each child. In it you could jot down specific reading skills that he needs work on, specific talents such as oral reading, and his particular interests in reading and extra projects.

Because your small reading groups would be so much more effective diagnostically, you would be able to skim the pupils' notebooks and set up other special-need groups to teach reading skills only to those who need them.

Since your special-need reading groups would be based on observation and testing, you could be more precise in meeting individual needs and much more economical with your own and your pupils' time.

There would be overlapping, as some children with greater remedial needs meet with many special-help groups. Those who don't need the extra help would be free to read independently and do special projects that interest them much more than drilling on what they already know.

In mathematics, a small group could work with great interest on problems at the board. Sometimes they could all share one problem and compete to think fast. Other times, each member of the small group could have a similar board problem, and the size of the group would make it practical for you to help all of them.

Newspaper Buzz Sessions

A buzz session about newspapers is a small group activity that can be used for many educational purposes. Over a period of a few days, select five or six newspaper articles that you think might be of interest to your pupils. The children's age will help you in this. Generally, younger children will not be interested in political, financial or foreign policy articles. Avoid stories about murders and gruesome details about disasters. Articles about sports, unusual medical discoveries, shortages of food, earthquakes or fires or anything that the child can relate to in some way will get the most responses.

For example, in just one newspaper the following provocative articles can be found:

"Central L. A. Blast Rips Up Whole Block"

"Fear Famine in India After Floods"

"Offshore Natural Gas Project is Costly But Vital to Future Supply"

"Friend Foils Holdup at Near North Shop"

Give one article to each buzz session group and ask them to read it and then discuss it for a few minutes. You can select a chairman for each group and have him read it aloud. After the group has finished its discussion, the chairman, with the help of the group, jots down a sentence or two summarizing the group's opinions and general comments.

To help start the discussions, you may wish to provide leaders with a choice of questions such as these:

What do you think about this?

Do you think something could have been done to prevent this?

Do you think it was handled well by the authorities concerned?

Do you know anything else about this?

The chairmen can choose the questions that would be appropriate for the article and add some of their own.

If time permits, it's fun to switch articles and repeat the process for each new article. If time is limited, duplicate one article so that each group discusses the same one. Then, each chairman reads aloud his summary report on the article. You can get some very different reactions to the same thing.

For older students, the activity can be handled competitively by having one group which does not have a discussion. These children will read the article and all of the buzz session reports and they will select the one report that is most interesting, shows the most effort and gives the most constructive opinions.

This activity is a welcome diversion late in the day when pupils are tired or restless. It gives them an opportunity to have a discussion about something topical, it provides practice in summarizing their opinions in a concise form and it is an experience in group cooperation.

One newspaper has classroom Activity Cards,* which can provide independent projects for individuals in all grades, free with classroom orders of the newspaper at half-price. This newspaper learning activity teaches language arts, social studies, mathematics and science, and it creates an interest in current events.

Letters to the Editor

You can extend the newspaper buzz session activity by selecting the article that has generated the most discussion and, hopefully, controversy. This is done best immediately afterward, while the discussion is still fresh in the pupils' minds.

When the buzz sessions are over, announce that as a result of all the interesting opinions you've heard, you believe that everyone should express these opinions to the newspaper editor in a letter.

Help pupils get started by writing the form of the letter on the chalkboard or overhead projector. You will find a letter form in the section on letter-writing in Chapter Two. Emphasize that the letters need not be long, but that they will be best when they give the writer's *own* opinion on the issue or event. Mention that

---

*Sun-Times Activity Cards, Chicago Sun-Times, School Services Division, Room 245, 401 N. Wabash Ave., Chicago, Ill. 60611.

any type of opinion or comment will be acceptable as long as it is sincerely felt and not profane.

This is just one example of how small group work can be extended or combined with effective large group activity.

A PRACTICAL WAY TO INDIVIDUALIZE
SCIENCE EXPERIENCES

As we all know, one of the most difficult things about experimenting in science is the obtaining of all the materials needed for each experiment. Some Learning Centers are beginning to assume responsibility for assembling science kits for classroom use. Many school science cabinets have available commercial experiment kits and some prepared by teachers to be shared.

Set up experiments for small groups to work on. In this way you will not need too many supplies or kits, and the pupils can interact and share experiences.

FLAG CELERY — A DEMONSTRATION
OF CONDUCTION

You may wish to try this popular demonstration:

MATERIALS: large *white* celery stalk with leaves turning white or yellow (If you must use green celery, take the inside stalk. You'll get dark green leaves instead of blue.)
red ink or food coloring
blue ink or food coloring
3 glasses half full of water
knife
spoon

PROCEDURE: Mix enough red and blue food coloring in two separate glasses of water to make a deeply-colored fluid. Half fill one glass with clear water. Cut ends of celery stalk obliquely. Split stalk end into three separate pieces almost up to top. Place one outside end of stalk in the red solution, the middle part in the clear water and the other outside end in the blue solution. Leave them in bright sunshine for at least a few hours. (The longer the better.)

RESULTS: The leaves should be red, white and blue. This method of coloring can also be used with lettuce leaves and white carnations.

An interesting variation is to try cutting one celery stalk at right angles and one obliquely. Observe which one transports liquids most quickly. Students will discover that celery strings are "pipes" or conducting tissue that brings moisture to the leaves. They will also learn that freshly-cut stems provide better conduction than dry or partially-sealed cuts. An oblique cut provides more absorptive surface. You can apply this to the care of cut flowers at home.

Science in a Shoebox*

This fascinating project has been planned and maintained weekly by an AAUW committee in cooperation with the Nichols Library. The purpose of the project is twofold: first, to interest children of grades one through eight in science as a supplement to formal learning in school; and, second, to encourage children in scientific reasoning.

There are five categories of scientific experiments† in different colored boxes, and there are five boxes in each category, making a total of twenty-five boxes. The categories are: Heat, Forces, Air and Sound, Optics, and Magnetism and Electricity.

Each box contains:

1. Library pocket and card (in lid).

2. Directions on heavy paper, list of contents and general instructions (in lid).

3. All items needed for all experiments within box (each box has eight to twelve experiments). Exception: the child must supply a flashlight for the Optics box and must supply water when necessary. All materials are

---

*Naperville American Association of University Women, Naperville, Ill.

† Some are really demonstrations.

safe for children if used according to instructions. Most materials are ordinary household objects.

4. Black cotton tape to tie lid to box.

Each box contains some experiments that are within the capabilities and understanding of children in the primary grades, as well as other experiments that are for older children in the intermediate or even junior high grades. In most cases, the detailed explanations and points for discussion at the end of the sets of experiments are meant for the older child.

If a child seems uncertain about which box to take home for the first time, the librarian is asked to encourage the younger child to try Heat first — that one has fewer experiments and they are rather easily performed. Optics is better suited to the older children while, at the same time, it also contains some simple scientific principles for the younger ones.

There is nothing new about most of the experiments, and many of them can be found in library books or textbooks on science. The main thing that makes this project unique is that all materials needed are supplied in the boxes and that it is a free service to the residents of the community.

Directions for the experiments have been written with the purpose of allowing the child to explore basic scientific principles unaided and, at the same time, to have fun. The criteria used for determining what kinds of experiments to use were: safety for the child, space limitation of the shoebox, illustration of basic scientific principles, capabilities of child's understanding and cost of supplies.

The committee hopes to plan additional experiments for a Set No. II and/or add new categories.

Science Materials for Individualizing

Science can be individualized with many of the good sets of materials for independent work. For example, *Parts of an Insect** is a complete lesson with a slide that fits in a microslide-viewer.

**Parts of an Insect,* Set III, National Teaching Aids, Inc., 120 Fulton Ave., Garden City Park, N.Y. 11040.

The teacher's guide has background information, specific teaching suggestions and suggested follow-up activities.

Intermediate elementary or junior high students will get a great deal from a fine series called the Basic Earth Science Program. These filmstrips, which are coordinated with 33-1/3 RPM records, can be used by individuals, small groups or the entire class. Audible and inaudible frame advances are provided for manual or automatic projectors. A good example of this series is called "Fossils."* A bibliography of related materials is also provided.

Independent learners can follow instructions on a cassette and learn to identify, remove and replace parts of a model representing a section of the human body. For instance, one model teaches all about the human ear.† The cassette asks frequent questions. The model set contains a key to the model, one audio cassette containing two lessons, two activity sheets and one test sheet on spirit duplicator masters and ten activity cards containing additional experiments and investigations.

KEYS TO ACHIEVING GROUP GOALS

Be aware of your goals. This is the best way to achieve them. Some of these goals are probably: good progress in learning concepts and skills, enthusiasm and improved attitudes toward learning, and better social behavior and cooperation.

Because there will be many times when a large group lesson is the most efficient way, don't hesitate to teach everyone at once. Initiating a new unit with a motivating session, giving instructions that everyone needs, showing a film of interest to all — the list could go on and on. Each child will learn, be enthused and want to cooperate by this type of a lesson.

---

*"Fossils," Series No. 6413, Basic Earth Science Program, Encyclopaedia Britannica Education Corporation, 425 N. Michigan Ave., Chicago, Ill. 60611. 1967. Produced by Encyclopaedia Britannica Films in cooperation with the American Geological Institute.

† "The Ear," (AM-113). A.J. Nystrom & Company, Field Enterprises Educational Corp., Chicago, Ill. 60618. 1972.

A Large Group Game*

Fifth and sixth grade students will enjoy a dictionary game in which each one has or shares a dictionary. The teacher chooses a word, pronounces it clearly and gives a sentence using the word in its context. The students compete to be the first to find the word, raise a hand, get called on, give the dictionary page number and select the correct dictionary entry to match the meaning for the sentence given. Some classes may compete as two teams working for points. A point can be given for the correct page number and entry, and a point can be deducted for an incorrect answer. This game will be good practice in discrimination of meanings.

When you can, work with children in small groups and committees. Simulations, remedial work, research and buzz sessions are a few examples of activities where you can better reach your group goals by breaking up the group into sub-groups.

In some cases, and only when you are able to do it without strain, work with individuals to reach these goals. There will be times when a certain child *needs* to be alone with you.

So, by being flexible and judging not only what you're teaching, but *who*, you can meet the last goal, which is important too: a satisfying teaching day for yourself.

INTERESTING INDIVIDUAL
LEARNING ACTIVITIES

"Perceptual Skills," the second part of the *Beginning to Learn*† series, is a multileveled program for developing visual perception in children from four-and-a-half through six years of age. It can be used independently with some teacher help or as a group lesson.

A good learning aid for kindergarten or first grade children is "What is My Color?"‡ matching cards. The color pictures and

---

*Florence Saipe, Armstrong School, 2111 W. Estes St., Chicago, Ill.

†Thelma G. Thurstone and David L. Lillie. *Beginning to Learn, Perceptual Skills*, No. 3-7040, Science Research Associates, Inc., 259 E. Erie St., Chicago, Ill. 60611, 1972.

‡ "What is My Color?" Educational Teaching Aids, A. Daigger & Co., 159 W. Kinzie St., Chicago, Ill. 60610.

the sentences are matched as reading and color identification practice. The color words and identifying part of the pictures are in separate pieces which are mixed up after each use.

"Trace-The-Letters Cards"* are flocked capital and lower case letters that may be used for initial instruction in letter formation, for review or for remediation in cases of confusion and reversal of letter forms. They are very good for independent practice after initial, directed experience to make sure that the child is correctly naming and tracing the letter.

If you have Spanish-speaking pupils, you may wish to use *Un Nombre Chistoso,* one of a series of beginning reading books.† It is attractive and colorful.

Kids' Stuff Math is a very useful book full of activities, games and ideas.‡ It includes numeration and number theory, sets and number concepts, whole numbers and integers, practice pages, fractional numbers, problem solving, measurement, geometry, probability, statistics and graphing.

Center Stuff for Nooks, Crannies and Corners will be invaluable for individualizing instruction.§ It is a teachers' guidebook full of easy-to-copy activity sheets that contain step-by-step directions for planning and implementing a wide variety of classroom learning centers. The three categories of centers are: Communications Skills Development Centers, Environmental Studies Centers and Quantitative Studies Centers.

The "Montessori play and learn™ programs"** are suitable for children from the ages of two-and-a-half through seven. Their learning apparatus teaches with complete audio, visual and tactile programs.

The Reading Readiness set contains an instruction book, a

---

* "Instructo Cursive Kinesthetic Trace-The-Letters Cards," No. 1229, McGraw-Hill, The Instructo Corporation, Paoli, Pa., 1973.

†Veronica Leal Gonzales, *Un Nombre Chistoso* (Berkeley, Calif.: Center for Open Learning and Teaching, Dolores Kohl Educational Foundation, 1974).

‡ Marjorie Frank, *Kids' Stuff Math* (P.O. Box 12522, Nashville, Tenn. 37212: Incentive Publications, Inc., 1974).

§ Imogene Forte, Mary Ann Pangle and Robbie Tupa, *Center Stuff for Nooks, Crannies and Corners* (P.O. Box 12522, Nashville, Tenn. 37212: Incentive Publications, Inc., 1973).

**"Montessori play and learn™ programs," Division of Dac Toymakers, Inc., Farmingdale, N.Y. 11735.

record, snap-out letters, sandpaper letters, phonetic words and matching phonetic pictures.

The Math Readiness program contains an instruction book, a record, sandpaper numerals, word cards, interlocking number rods and colored discs.

These programs seem to be very useful for young children to work on independently with guidance.

"Initial Sounds in Spanish"* will be helpful in teaching Spanish-speaking students to read English. The word-picture cards have a picture on the front and the name word on the back in both Spanish and English. Each is identified with a special code so that they may be arranged in a variety of ways — presenting various concepts in classification.

Fifth and sixth graders will enjoy writing individual, one page newspapers each week.† They will make up their own names for their papers, act as their own editors and handwrite their papers in manuscript writing. The papers will consist of foreign, United States and local news, but they will avoid sensational or gossip items. The local news can include stories about school, weather and sports. No maps or pictures will be in the papers — just reporting. Students will keep up with world and local news, use maps to check locations and get practice in writing concise news stories in this individual activity. Interesting social studies or language displays can be made from the newspapers.

MOTIVATING WITH FREEDOM

There is nothing more stifling to a child than the lock-step rigidity of "covering the book." If a district or a principal expects you to cover specific curriculum content or certain books for each child, and this is becoming rare, there are different ways to do it.

Encourage independent projects, experiments and research of all kinds that go beyond the text. The best independent project of all develops from a child's questions or curiosity.

Some children must have the freedom to work on their own,

---

* "Initial Sounds in Spanish," No. ID 2000, Ideal School Supply Co., Oak Lawn, Ill. 60453.

† Florence Saipe, Armstrong School, 2111 W. Estes St., Chicago, Ill.

even if they do the same work with the same book as the class. Instead of having them join in a class lesson on a specific chapter, allow these few pupils to read ahead and work independently.

Be enthusiastic about students' ideas and encourage them to strike out on their own. Try to reduce children's tension about their work by being uncritical of their projects as long as efforts are made. Once you have been accepting and interested in their reports, you can make corrections and suggestions.

All children need to know that their teacher cares about what they are doing, and they work better if their lessons are checked. Some types of questions may be answered and checked independently with answer sheets, but pupils must know that their work is going to be read by their teacher.

Independent projects are a must for gifted children, and they are interesting for all pupils. Never allow a gifted child to sit day after day doing the same thing in a book. Vary his work with special study on a topic for a written or oral report. A diorama can require days of research and study for a student to achieve correct costumes, background and realia to portray a historical period.

Bright children, even more than others, need responsibility. They crave a project to do, something that they alone are expected to accomplish. They sense their ability and they want to use it. There is a terrible frustration when a child isn't given or allowed to create his own special activities. Whether it's measuring everything in sight using the metric system, or writing a pupil's handbook in a foreign language, gifted children need more to do, and they need work of a *different quality*. Just increasing the quantity of an assignment will not be satisfying or enriching. If it is challenging to pupils and also useful, you have achieved the ultimate.

One very real way that gifted students can feel useful and motivated is by pupil tutoring. This is discussed further in the section called "How to Use Pupil Teachers" in Chapter One.

Allow gifted students to help you in many ways. Do not have guilt feelings and think that you are exploiting them and that they are doing your work. The good feelings they get from being responsible and useful will motivate them to learn more and to become better people.

Give each child in your class the feeling of freedom. They all need the freedom to do more, to investigate, to help each other and to question everything.

LETTING THE COMMUNITY TEACH

There is so much to learn in each community, big or small, that we mustn't waste it because of the possible difficulty in getting to it. We cannot assume that all parents have the time, inclination, patience or transportation to make use of the available community resources.

Plan your trips carefully so that they will be more than pleasure outings, as trips are too expensive and time-consuming to be just that. A good educational trip will be pleasurable because of its inherent interest.

A trip to a nature center is always better if you have a special guide or a very knowledgeable science teacher to point out interesting flora and fauna. Otherwise, the trip can deteriorate into just a picnic. If you cannot obtain a guide, spend a great deal of your time on the exhibits planned for you inside the nature center itself.

A trip to a museum can be educational or it can be no more than a tiring scurrying here and there, and it all depends upon your planning. If you are willing and able to scout the exhibits ahead of time you can plan every move you make and have an extremely valuable visit. Since few of us have the time to do that,. the next best thing is to write the museum for its guide book or floor plan. One museum publishes a special guide with general information, floor plans, an index to exhibits and a subject index.* If you think through where you will go and about how much time to allow for the main exhibits, your students will learn much about the topics you are all working on. It is best to concentrate on two or three main things to see, and allow a little free time at the end of the tour to just browse.

If your visit will not include subjects you are currently studying you may wish to review some past units, or intrigue students with subjects that are coming up soon.

---

*Teacher's Guide to the Museum of Science and Industry, Museum of Science and Industry, E. 57th St. and Lake Shore Dr., Chicago, Ill.

If the day is spent just looking at all the exhibits, regardless of what you are studying in school, try to avoid things that your pupils will not understand such as very technical chemical posters for young children. Spend your time on exhibits that will interest and teach your students.

Have adequate parent help on field trips, as it is impossible to have pupils learn from and enjoy a trip when you are upset from chasing them, trying to keep them together or looking for lost stragglers. Allow enough time for washroom stops to avoid having individuals leave the group. If this becomes absolutely necessary, an adult must accompany the child while you handle their small group. The ideal number of pupils per group is five or less for each adult. Many parents love these tours and make excellent leaders. Give them fact sheets if you wish them to be of extra help to the students. A small group enables leaders to answer questions effectively and to discuss exhibits so they can be heard.

Use public libraries for a place to visit, and children can bring their own library cards. Plan for this ahead of time, as it is not a good idea for you to be responsible for all of their materials. (I tried it, and it gets very wearing and expensive.) If children are studying individual topics, it is fun for them to search for materials in a different library, in addition to their own school library. Show pupils how to find books, magazines, pamphlets, records and pictures. Some libraries have extensive picture files available for loaning.

Visit zoos, factories, post offices, courtrooms and other schools; and take students to special community events. Plan these visits in advance, and make sure that your group will be welcome. This requires telephoning, reservations and the adjusting of trip times to the hours and convenience of your hosts. It will be well worthwhile.

Exploit your community volunteers. Make use of all of the wonderful, willing people who want to share their knowledge and their time. They can be your richest resource if you plan well. Let them know your exact needs and the vocabulary level and interests of your pupils. Do not expect volunteers to know how to adjust their material to your students on the spot, so help them to prepare suitable lessons. Encourage resource people to show realia, films, slides etc. If they give lectures, ask them to keep them short and to have frequent question and answer sessions.

Your community is rich in fascinating resources, and there is a great deal there that you couldn't possibly teach in your classroom. Use all the help you can get and go to see everything you can.

An original experiment in making the city a classroom is "Metro High," designed by the Urban Research Corporation for the Chicago Board of Education.* The Chicago High School for Metropolitan Studies follows the graduation requirements of the school system, interpreting them loosely. English may be *Tales of Horror.* "Metro High" rents space at 525 S. Dearborn Street in Chicago, but its classes can also be found in Shedd Aquarium, DePaul University, Lincoln Park Zoo and Malcom X College. Several businesses run classes for them. Illinois Bell Telephone Company, for example, teaches electronics using its own personnel and its own equipment. Stockbrokers from A.G. Becker and Company teach finance.

An interesting article in the *Science Activities* magazine tells about a program in Rochester, New York, in which scientists from industry have provided consultant services to seven grade schools.†

These consultants, many of them from the local American Chemical Society, are released from their jobs and other responsibilities at Kodak, Xerox and DuPont on a one-half-day-a-week basis to work with children and teachers in areas of pupil interests.

Guests from industry, service groups and the professions could be reached by phoning or writing: 1) local professional societies, 2) parents of students, 3) local volunteer groups and 4) local fire and police departments.

EXAMPLES OF EFFECTIVE
INDIVIDUALIZED LEARNING

I read the following paragraph written by a child, and I got curious about it:

My gourd is bumby and my gourd is 9½ inches arond

---

*Lois Wille, "They Won't Leave School! Where Students Hate to See the School Year End," *The Chicago Daily News*, Oct. 20, 1971, pp. 1, 8.

† Robert G. Dyment, "Science Consultants for the Inner City," *Science Activities*, Apr., 1971, Vol. 5, No. 3, pp. 34-7, 55-6.

*my gourd weigh 11 washers and 4 poker chips and 5
inches up and down my gourd it weigh 5 erasers.*

A willing little girl explained it all to me very proudly. She
showed me a balancing scale and demonstrated how individuals
work with it:*

BALANCING

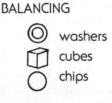

washers
cubes
chips

Figure 3-1

She pointed to the above sign with the symbols and then
began to weigh various objects, adding objects until the scale
balanced. Gourds, washers, cubes and poker chips were all used.
The child told me that when the objects were balanced, the
children wrote up what they had accomplished. Sometimes the
results were written up in a paragraph, and other times an equal
sign was used. It looked like fun.

This same teacher had another fine activity for individuals.
There were three signs each with an envelope below them:

USING MY EARS   USING MY EYES   SORT THESE CARDS.
                                          SHOW YOUR TEACHER.

Figure 3-2

The children in this multi-age first and second grade class
had the following cards for sorting. (You may wish to add a third
envelope with the sign "USING MY EARS *AND* MY EYES.")

a clock ticking	a kitten purring
the wind howling	the patter of rain
a squeaking wheel	dishes clattering
beds of pansies	a fluffy white cloud

---

*Lisbie Goss, Central School, District No. 39, Wilmette, Ill.

wreaths of flowers	a ball bouncing
the blue sky	a streak of lightning
snow on the ground	a pretty fawn
bells ringing	a streaker streaking
a dog barking	your mom yelling

a rooster crowing

Plastic covered large index cards can be used in another good activity for first and second graders to do on their own.* Children will copy the following sentences, filling in the correct verbs in the blanks. Once the sentences are completed and copied, pupils will cut them apart and put the sentences in correct order so they make a sensible story. Children paste the sentences in order on another sheet of paper and draw an appropriate picture at the bottom of the page. You can compose your own sentences for the age or interests of your students, or add to those given here to make enough for a longer story:

(These sentences have been numbered for your convenience, but the numerals will not appear on the cards. A few more sentences will make the story more complete.)

"Some day," said Tommy, "we will be _____ and not just _____." (6)

galloped	galloping	gallops
pretended	pretending	pretends

They saw Penny and Pam trotting their ponies and _____ them to jump. (3)

taught	teach	teaching

Tommy and Danny were _____ near the barn. (1)

play	playing	played

Tommy and Danny _____ to ride, too. (5)

want	wanted	wants

They _____ up on top of the fence. (2)

climb	climbs	climbed

The ponies _____ again and again. (4)

jumped	jumps	jumping

---

*Lisbie Goss, Central School, District No. 39, Wilmette, Ill.

The teacher who used these activities had an impressive and courteous way of maintaining the quiet discipline necessary for effective individualizing. She thanked her first and second graders for being so quiet in their reading and thinking while she worked one-to-one with some people.

Primary pupils will enjoy and benefit from an activity in which they paste colored magazine pictures on charts under appropriate descriptive words.* Discuss the fact that some pictures may fit well in more than one category, so more than one answer can be correct. For example, in the group of words describing pictures in the chart below — *car, motorcycle, airplane* and *leopard* could all be used under *FAST* or *VERY FAST*. Tell children to make a choice and it will probably be correct.

SLOW	FAST	VERY FAST
ship bear	car motorcycle	airplane leopard
LIGHT	HEAVY	VERY HEAVY
flower	dog	car

Figure 3-3

One teacher of first and second graders uses a provocative question to inspire individual and small group investigations.† He asks, "What are you curious about?" During the discussion period after his question, he jots down the pupils' answers, but does not try to talk about the topics. He encourages small groups working in the library with his help to find out answers and information on the questions, using all kinds of audio-visual materials. The size of the group depends on the interest shown. Some typical answers to the teacher's question are given below:

fire   how paint is made   how airplanes fly
how a colt could come out of its mother when it's so big
how people are made

—————————
    *Marlys Washburn, Central School, District No. 39, Wilmette, Ill.
   † Steve Pritikin, Central School, District No. 39, Wilmette, Ill.

CHECKLIST

* Vary the size of your learning groups with the activity or the skill that is being taught.
* Group and regroup as needed, and avoid rigid ability groups.
* Use small groups to teach individuals.
* Encourage independent science work with kits and audio-visual materials.
* Achieve group goals by being aware of your goals and by being flexible.
* Give children the freedom to work independently at their own speed.
* Be uncritical of student projects at first as long as efforts are made.
* Expect a different kind of achievement from your gifted students — not just a greater quantity of work.
* Avoid routine assignments by giving a different quantity and kind of work to children with different needs.
* Give responsibility and a chance to be useful, especially to the very bright.
* Reward excellent independent work of gifted pupils by having them teach their projects as lessons to other classes.
* Use all of your community's resources to teach your pupils.
* Plan field trips carefully to maximize their effectiveness.
* Expect adequate parent help for field trips so that children can tour and learn in small groups.
* Make effective use of community volunteers by communicating your pupils' needs to them.
* Provide opportunities for individuals to weigh, measure, discriminate and investigate.

4

Team Teaching Approaches
To Individualization

There are many different names for the various types of elementary classes. What they are called is not half as important as what is done for the children.

The most familiar teaching unit is still the self-contained classroom with one teacher, or a teacher with an aide. But there are many other methods being tried.

Team teaching is the most widely used other method, and its meaning varies from school to school. Team teaching is the pooling of time and efforts of two or three teachers who work together as a unit with a large group of students. Teachers' aides and student teachers also usually act as part of a team.

In the usual form of team teaching, each team member teaches all subjects except reading and mathematics to his own home room. In reading and mathematics, all of the children are regrouped by ability and team members usually teach only one level of ability in each of these subjects. So, a teacher's reading group and mathematics group will probably be composed of some pupils from other home rooms.

Pupils can benefit from team teaching when it is done well. They can have their individual needs met by this type of ability grouping, and they have an opportunity to work with more than one teacher and with children from other classes. Because of this, in some cases they share more ideas and talents and the children are not held back by slower students or overawed by brighter ones.

With this kind of team teaching, although the class members will change for reading and mathematics, the class size is not radically different. Team teachers often plan trips and special events together. The teachers can prepare one lesson in reading and one in mathematics, rather than three or more in each subject. Because of these things, teachers can benefit too.

Another, rarer, type of team teaching is one that uses ability grouping in reading and mathematics, but does something more. In this type, the teachers pool their efforts in all subjects, partly based on their own abilities and wishes. For instance, if one teacher has a talent for art, but sings like a bullfrog, she teaches all of the art, or divides it with one other team member. The teachers who know music, or the ones who are able to sing, divide the three classes and teach them together. This kind of flexibility lessens the likelihood of inept teaching by a teacher who hates, or is ignorant in, one particular subject.

Another type of class grouping is the multi-age ungraded teaching program, which can be taught by a team or in a self-contained classroom. This, as well as team teaching, will be discussed further.

This chapter will tell you how to teach individually by using flexible groupings. It will give examples of effective procedures, and it will show you how to avoid busywork by using pupils' interests to reach group objectives.

HOW TO TEACH INDIVIDUALLY BY USING FLEXIBLE GROUPINGS

By grouping children according to ability and interest rather than age, and by providing teachers and aides for each group, pupils can learn as rapidly as they are able in each subject. Gifted children move swiftly and also are able to help their peers. Slower learners receive extra help and go at their own pace with no risk of failure. Removal of grade levels helps in this. Teaching of this type demands individualization of instruction and small group teaching. It can be the very best method of all if a careful check is made on each pupil's progress. It can also be the very worst way if children work too much on their own with too little guidance and instruction.

Team teaching can use another kind of flexibility in grouping in every subject; not by the child's ability, (except in reading and mathematics) but by the type of activity planned for the day. For example, two teachers may conduct a lecture-demonstration or film together for all three classes, or one could do it alone — to allow one or more other teachers to work with one child at a time; or with a tiny group on a special experiment that needs individual attention; or to take a few pupils on a short trip related to their projects; or do remedial work with individuals. The size and the make-up of a study group would vary from day to day, based on the particular activity planned and on the needs of pupils.

If one teacher works well with children as they do experiments, she would be given the freedom to teach a small, manageable group, with very little supplies and equipment needed. Not only the size of the group would be a factor, but also the individual talents and interests of each team teaching member. If one teacher speaks well to a large group, she might be the one to lead a discussion or a demonstration for everyone. Another team member might specialize in setting up mechanical equipment such as tape recorders, microprojectors and film projectors.

This type of teaching, with its extreme flexibility, taps the talents of each teacher and makes the best use of each team member's time. There may be a day when a resource person comes to visit, and one teacher takes charge while the others are freed to get materials ready for lessons or to meet for a planning session.

The advantages of this flexible team teaching have been stated. Its only disadvantage lies in its need for extra planning, but the very nature of the process allows some free time for two of the three teachers once in a while. At times the class group will be large, but only when the nature of the activity permits it.

An important prerequisite for successful team teaching is compatibility of personalities and teaching goals, so these must be considered.

EXAMPLES OF EFFECTIVE PROCEDURES

Two very compatible team teachers have provided the following ideas which they are using in their fourth and fifth grade class.*

---

*Marie Rolston and Kenneth Scharmann, Central School, District No. 39, Wilmette, Ill.

Their multi-age group has forty-eight pupils, who are divided into two separate groups for one hour each day, based on their ability to do independe   work, not on age. The independent workers are called the "Blah, Blah, Blahs," and within this group there are two sub-groups. Twelve children are able to work completely on their own on self-chosen research topics. The other twelve work on independent study projects chosen from a teacher-selected list of topics.

The other group of pupils, called the "Philadelphia 76'rs," work with a teacher or student teacher on developing independent learning skills. They learn how to take notes, use a library, work with an index and table of contents and they discuss current events. When these pupils work on reports they are closely guided.

In a typical learning session, one teacher might be in the Learning Center, available to help independent workers. The other teacher might be in one classroom with those independent pupils working there. A student teacher might be working on study skills in the other classroom with the "Philadelphia 76'rs."

When needed, the teacher helps pupils to outline their topics, define them, plan what materials they will need and answer the question, "What will you end up with in this report?" as well as give encouragement and help. Reports are checked on with checklists. Questions and checks such as "Show us something" and "What did you get?" keep the pupils motivated by their teachers' interest.

Practice is given in using encyclopedias and all other research skills. One interesting exercise is shown below:

WHERE CAN YOU FIND OUT

the atomic symbol for oxygen? _____

_____

about Madame Curie?   _____

_____

information about Niels Bohr? _____

_____

This class has its weekly spelling list provided by two different pupils each week. The words come from work units or are some the children would like to learn. At times the teachers must take some words from the list because they are too difficult. Some typical pupil-chosen words are: Albuquerque, encyclopedia and Afghanistan.

Bulletin Board Ideas

These team teachers use their bulletin boards as teaching devices. One board has the following titles over a large collection of numbered air mail letters:

Where did these letters come from?
How many miles did they come to Chicago?

Individuals can work with the air mail letters in their spare time. They check the postmark to answer the first question, and then they use an atlas to answer the second. Their answers are numbered to match the numerals on the letters, and they are checked by the teachers.

One bulletin board is an example of these teachers' interest in affective education. It is called the "Let It All Hang Out" board. A large sheet of white paper is stapled to the bulletin board and the students are encouraged to write anything they wish on it, including their feelings. At the start of this board, after an off-color beginning, it was limited to all other kinds of graffiti.

Their current events bulletin board is titled "Most Likely to Become History," an interesting approach which encourages discrimination of important items. Each letter in the title is made of both black construction paper and newspaper, and the black letter is placed so that it looks like a shadow of the newspaper letter.

Another board is devoted to individual biographies. Each one tells about birth details, ambitions, hobbies, friends, favorite sports, colors, foods and TV programs. The teachers wrote their own biographies too. The title of the board is:

W
W H O'S
O
?

Goal Sheet

One sixth grade teacher uses the following goal sheet for his students.* He began it first on a daily basis, and then they worked

---

*Thomas L. Berenz and Susan Huster, Howard Junior High School, District No. 39, Wilmette, Ill.

up to a weekly contract. The students fill out the sheets for themselves and the teacher looks at them.

Younger pupils may be able to use this goal sheet if it is used selectively. Some children may be able to fill out part of it, and others may not be able to do it at all. This is something that can be tried early in the school year for those able to do part of it. It can be discontinued if it is too difficult and tried again later.

GOAL SHEET

NAME _____DATE _____

MY GOAL FOR TODAY

READING   TITLE _____
             P.
MATH: BOOK _____
             P.
LANGUAGE:

SOCIAL STUDIES:

SCIENCE:

ANYTHING ELSE:

Figure 4-1

AVOIDING BUSYWORK — USING PUPILS' INTERESTS TO REACH GROUP OBJECTIVES

Children *know* when they're just being kept busy, and they become sluggish and uninterested. Vary assignments for different students and give them importance in the children's minds.

If a book has questions or assignments at the end of each chapter, use some of them as a way of checking on understanding. Give frequent oral and written quizzes so the child feels motivated to keep going and to do his very best. It is seldom productive to use all of the questions at the end of each chapter, as they can become very boring to do if used routinely. Select some of the best, and give extra credit if pupils choose to do more. A notebook can be kept by pupils, recording the chapters read, questions answered, extra credits and quizzes completed.

Much of what has been started in many multi-age classes is very similar to an innovation in teaching called the *open school,* based on a system now being used in England. Its main element is freedom of curriculum. The teacher selects and organizes activities using the children's interests. This method individualizes instruction, allowing much experimentation and observation. Basic subjects are still taught, but in different combinations with others, and with a new freedom and interest for pupils and teachers. A book called *Inside the Primary School** describes the open school as it is being developed in England.

Many classes here which begin with the open school method find that it has much of value, but must be modified. Pupil interest is still a major factor, but it is combined with a more traditional curriculum.

Every section of this book deals with some kind of independent study because it is so important, especially to bright students. These children can be with the class on a topic, and yet be studying it in depth on their own. They may start with the unit and have it lead them to other, different subjects that they want to learn. Education is more and more allowing students to learn what interests them, without allowing them to limit themselves to just that. Forced study of topics that do not hold students' interest gives diminishing returns.

Try to allow students to go off on tangents, even if the class is studying one topic. If a pupil finds something that interests him, let him explore it, as the freedom to use the library for research will stimulate a child. Hopefully, he will continue to search for material and knowledge in his home library and he will talk to his parents and other adults. Free children to find out things on their own.

Team teaching and multi-age grouping methods will be only as effective as the teachers who use them and the organizational approach they use. Team teaching should not be used as a way to cut staff and enlarge classes. It must be a way to achieve better instruction for each child.

---

*John Blackie, *Inside the Primary School* (London, England: Her Majesty's Stationery Office, 1969).

CHECKLIST

* Use team teaching at its best by ability grouping in reading and mathematics and flexible planning to utilize the team's time and talents.
* Group children doing independent work by their ability to take responsibility and by their study and research skills.
* Check extra carefully on students' daily progress in ungraded classes.
* Teach with your bulletin boards by using them for motivation, self-expression and to stimulate pupils' curiosity and independent study.
* Set goals *with* your students, not for them.
* Diagnose individuals' needs in every way possible, by testing and observation.
* Avoid busywork by giving individual assignments, with students keeping records of their work and extra credits.
* Use pupils' interests to reach group objectives in any way within the framework of traditional curriculum requirements.
* Allow students to explore subjects related to the regular topic if they are interested in them.
* Use team teaching to improve instruction, not to cut staff and enlarge classes.

5

Learning with Games and Game-like Activities

Teaching with games can be very stimulating and effective. A game can start with two children and end with many pupils playing in small groups by taking turns. This type of enthusiasm that children have for games can be used to teach them many things. The increased enjoyment and attention shown by youngsters will convince you that educational games are valuable teaching tools.

This chapter will encourage you to use pupil creativity and research in constructing your own educational games. It will also include some suggestions for good teaching games and for activities that *seem* like games. A practice activity, *Metric Mysteries,* is given. You will learn how to individualize with bulletin board projects that teach. Also, a sample game, *Camera Safari,* is provided for you, complete and ready to use in your classroom.

USING PUPIL CREATIVITY AND RESEARCH IN CONSTRUCTING GAMES

Use the help of all of your students in designing and constructing games. It will give them a worthwhile project to work on, provide them the satisfaction of helping you and save you a great deal of time.

It is especially valuable for you to expect gifted pupils to help you compose educational games. You may begin the process by suggesting a game idea related to a unit or subject you may be beginning. Have your pupils start helping with routine question cards. Allow time for frequent large and small group meetings in which you discuss the game and its goals. Some of the children may surprise you by inventing a better game than you started with, so be receptive to new ideas and to changes in the structure of the game. The creativity and imagination used in devising and improving games can be a challenging education.

Games teaching subject matter require extensive research to get correct facts. These facts may be needed for spaces on a board game, for answer cards or answer sheets. This hunt for information will be very important to your pupils, because they know that it will be used for something they are going to be working with. Small groups of pupils can be assigned to different trade books, encyclopedias, textbooks, filmstrips and other sources. Arm them with notebooks, pencils and specific topics to look up. Encourage youngsters to rewrite the facts in their own words, to write down the information on their sources for a bibliography and to jot down short notes on the most important things they find. Children will know that this is not busywork because they are creating a game that they are going to play.

SUGGESTIONS FOR GOOD EDUCATIONAL GAMES

Many, many good educational games are available, and those mentioned here are only a sampling of the newest and the best that I was able to find. You will discover good games for your classroom by exploring your district's Materials Center and finding all that it offers for your use. Some sources of game ideas are books, catalogs, other teachers, stores and university curriculum centers. The best way to get a variety of good games is to borrow from your Materials Center, which can afford to invest in many good books and games for the use of its district's teachers. If you must order your own games, study and try them out ahead of time, if possible, because budgets for individual teachers are low, and you may not get many.

Rain on My Umbrella*

The following game is one of the many good ones that can be

---

*Delwyn G. Schubert, Ph. D., editor, *Reading Games that Teach*, Book 1: Readiness, Visual Discrimination, Auditory Discrimination (Monterey Park, Calif.: Creative Teaching Press, Inc., 1968), Game #4.

found in the series, *Reading Games that Teach*. This game was taken from Book 1: Readiness, Visual Discrimination, Auditory Discrimination.

Grade Level: K-1

Purpose: Letter recognition skill.

Material: Tag board, sheet of heavy clear plastic, wax pencil.

Group Size: Individual, or small group.

Steps:

1. Draw an opened umbrella on the tag board. Section the surface of the umbrella into 26 parts. Put one upper case letter in each section.

2. Draw 26 raindrops above the umbrella. Put a lower case letter in each raindrop.

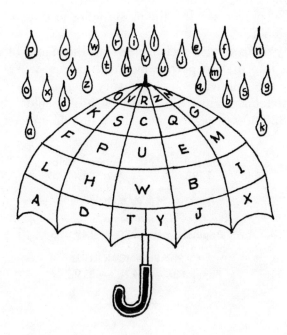

Figure 5-1

3. Cover the tag board with a sheet of clear plastic.

4. Ask children to find where the raindrops will fall.*
   A wax pencil may be used to draw a line on the plastic from the upper case letter to the same letter in lower case, showing where the raindrops will fall.

When the teacher checks these lines and praises the child for correctly matching the upper and lower case letters, this letter recognition game will be even more valuable. The plastic is then wiped off and the game is ready to be used again.

Game of States†

This is a highly entertaining and educative game for two, three or four players, and it can be used in the middle and upper grades.

It teaches the location of each of the states, the capital city, and its important industries and products which the players buy and sell.

The object of the game is to buy a product in one state and haul it on a truck to another state where you try to sell it at a profit. The player who has the most money at the end of the game is the winner.

Fifty state cards, each containing the name of a state and valuable information pertaining to it, are used. The game also includes the following: four delivery trucks, one each of four colors; sixteen product discs, four each of a color, matching the trucks; $20,000 in play money and a double spinner.

Annexed in   **Entered Union**
1898   **Aug. 21, 1959**

HAWAII
"Aloha State"
Population — 1970 — 748,575

CAPITAL — HONOLULU
Population — 1970 — 319,784

Figure 5-2

_____

* so letters will match.

† Game of States, Copyright 1960 by Milton Bradley Company.   Reproduced with permission of Milton Bradley Company, Springfield, Mass. 01101.

The principal products made or grown in the states in real life are usually trucked to other states and sold there in the open market. However, in this game, so that all players have an equal chance to make money, each player sells his products to his opponents in one state and buys them back again when the discs are delivered to another state. Each time a product is bought or sold, the price for it is found by spinning the BLUE MONEY DIAL. To add zest to the game, the players may speculate when buying or selling.

The state cards may also be used in playing a STATE QUIZ GAME for any number of players. One player, who acts as Quizmaster or Teacher, holds the cards and asks questions of other players. For instance, he may ask, "What is the capital of Kentucky?" or "Which state is called the SOONER state?" etc. When a player answers the question correctly, he gets that card, and the player collecting the largest number of cards is the winner. Only one fact on a card (such as capitals) is used for each game.

Multifacto Producto*

Both games, *Multifacto* and *Producto*, have been designed to help students of grades four through nine develop proficiency with multiplication facts.

Producto can be adapted to groups of two through six players or to the entire class. The materials include game boards made from duplicating masters and number cards.

Directions for playing *Producto:*

The wild cards are taken out of the deck. To select a caller, each player draws a card from the deck. The player with the highest number is the caller. Each player takes one game board different from the others and writes in random order the numerals one through ten in the squares at the top and the left side of his board. Squares have pictures of different objects.

The caller shuffles the cards and places them face down in a pile. He then draws one card at a time and calls out a product. Each player should write that product in the squares corresponding to its factors. For instance, if 12 were called, each player should write 12 in the proper squares for 6 x 2, 2 x 6, 4 x 3 and

---

*"Multifacto Producto," Wayne H. Peterson, Scott Foresman Math Aid, 1971. Scott, Foresman and Co., Glenview, Ill.

3 x 4. For 6 x 2, each player would find 6 in the column at the left and then go right to the column under 2 and write 12 in that square.

The first player to correctly fill in all the squares showing the same object calls out the name of that object. If he filled in all the squares showing trees, he would call out "trees." He then must give the ten multiplication facts he used to fill in those squares. If another player proves he has made a mistake, the first student is disqualified and the game goes on until there is a winner.

The caller may use the multiplication table given in the instruction sheet for reference in checking the winner.

The *Multifacto* game, for two to four players, is based on an understanding of factors and multiples. Students should have some familiarity with factoring numbers not greater than 100 and with listing multiples of numbers not greater than 10. The first player to play all of his cards wins the game.

*EDUVIZ™ Science Bingo**

EDUVIZ consists of colorful "Bingo-Type" cards designed to teach vocabulary and concepts of classification. It provides an excellent motivational and reinforcement tool. Motivation is stimulated through a series of innovating "fun activities" while identification is reinforced through auditory and visual stimuli. EDUVIZ is excellent for use among small groups — with the students, in many cases, administering the activities themselves or to each other.

This game offers an aid for the introduction of units in the middle grades and as review and reinforcement for the upper grades.

EDUVIZ is an excellent multiple choice pretest or post-test in which the poor reader is aided by the use of the illustrations and the clues which are read aloud by the teacher.

Some general concepts presented in "The Plant Kingdom" show that:

1. Plants may be classified according to structure and function.

2. The simpler plants are those which have few parts and reproduce by division, budding or spores.

---

*"EDUVIZ™ Science Bingo," ID 5700, "The Plant Kingdom," Ideal School Supply Co., Oak Lawn, Ill. 60453.

3. Flowering plants have more complicated organs of reproduction.

4. Most seed-bearing plants and cone-bearing plants are specially adapted to land environments.

5. Man is dependent on plants for most of his requirements and luxuries.

6. Through the study and understanding of plants, man hopes to improve his environment.

Learning Objectives:

1. to teach science vocabulary
2. to teach concepts of classifications
3. to provide reinforcement through auditory and visual stimuli
4. to motivate learning

For *Science Bingo*, the game includes 36 Clue Cards, 16 "Bingo-Type" Playing Cards and 320 Playing Tokens. As the teacher reads aloud each clue card, the student covers the picture on one square of his "Bingo-Type" playing card. The pictures are covered with the plastic discs or playing tokens. When a player has covered all the pictures in a row of six squares, he raises his hand. If the row covered contains six correct answers from the clues which were read, the player (or his team) receives ten points. The player (or team) receiving the most points is the winner of the game.

CLUE CARD

Plant Kingdom

D

CLUE:

A thallophyte without chlorophyll

ANSWER:

FUNGUS

Figure 5-3

92425

Other games that can be played with the clue cards are *Eduviz Rummy* and *Advanced Eduviz Rummy.*

GOMSTON™ — A Polluted City*

This is a simulation game on ecology in which the entire class participates. The game is excellent for any student in fifth grade through high school, and it will be a valuable teaching tool in all areas of the curriculum.

Each member of the class becomes a citizen of Gomston — a typical modern community with environmental problems. For example, Gomston suffers from air pollution due to gaseous emissions from its steel mill, electric generation station and its many privately owned automobiles. Unrestricted leaf and trash burning also add to the air pollution problem which is causing unhealthy and unsafe living conditions. Wildlife is being destroyed and property values are going down. Water pollution is at an all-time high, mainly as a result of the actions of the industrial and municipal concerns, the use of phosphates and poor farming practices in the area.

The primary objectives of the simulation are:

1. to generate a concern and understanding of the problems of environmental degradation in Gomston.

2. to provide for consideration of possible solutions to these environmental problems and the effects of same.

3. to create a classroom situation in which the problems of environmental degradation can be analyzed.

4. that the insights gained in the Gomston situation foster an understanding and awareness of the "real world" situation to an increased degree.

The simulation kit includes a 36-frame filmstrip with accompanying tape cassette, an overhead projection transparency map of Gomston, students' copies of the maps of Gomston, before and after pictures of the city, a sample daily lesson plan, student role

---

*"GOMSTON™ — A Polluted City," ID 3055, Norman S. Warns, Jr. 1973, Ideal School Supply Co., Oak Lawn, Ill. 60453.

sheets, student worksheets, quiz sheets, evaluation sheets, twelve committee signs, a teacher's manual and a storage box.

For effectiveness, any simulation should have certain characteristics. These characteristics vary to some extent in relation to the time and facilities available, the experience the students have had with simulations, and to a lesser extent, the level and competence of the students. *Gomston* is a simulation in which level and competence should not be major determining factors. Relating to competence, many so-called "under-achievers" seem much more imaginative and creative than the so-called "high-achievers." Perhaps this is because the poorer students are less textbook oriented, less able to "psych out" what the teacher is looking for and thus more creative in an open situation such as *Gomston*. Likewise, the concepts of the problems are decided upon by each individual class, not by the publisher, author or teacher. Therefore, this simulation should not be too complex or too simple for the individual class.

The following characteristics are important to the success of this simulation:

1. Roles played by the students must be specific.
2. The method of decision-making must be specific (voting rules).
3. The framework in which the roles and decisions are to be effected must be specified.

To insure that the roles are played realistically, each group is given a list of goals. The goals are printed on the back of each committees' nameplate.

ACTIVITIES THAT SEEM LIKE GAMES

There are many classroom activities that are so interesting and enjoyable for students (and teachers) that they seem like games. Use them as often as you can.

Comic Strip Stories

Select and save up comic strips that are particularly amusing or interesting and use them for a large group activity or for individuals. The comic strips can stimulate a creative story, or they can be used to provide the impetus to a pupil so he can write a paragraph summarizing what has happened in the comic strip.

Although creative activity is always looked for, we should also value the opportunities we can develop for language practice. Any type of written expression in which the pupil has to summarize or organize his thoughts in writing is very much needed.

The humor and colorful pictures of comic strips will add fun to this writing practice. Keep the strips for future use.

Plays

Children of all ages love plays, and they enjoy performing in them and seeing them. You will be pleased at their enthusiasm if you initiate a play-writing and performing activity.

The best way to motivate this is to have a few children play in a *very* short skit that does not take too much rehearsal time. Then the group will still be excited about the idea of giving another play.

You can generate a great deal of excitement by suggesting that the class writes its own play. Give the students time to discuss plot ideas and characters, and then postpone the final decisions until the children have time to think about the play.

The next session, use everyone's ideas for the type of play, the title and the story. When you get at *least* two possibilities, have the class vote between the play ideas. Then turn the discussion to planning as many characters as possible, so that all of the children can participate in the production in their own way.

End the session by calling for volunteers to write the play, act in it, help direct it, make costumes, construct and paint sets, make and sell tickets and write and draw advertising posters. You'll find that everyone will want to participate in some way, and the volunteering can even become frantic.

An easy way to plan the beginning stages is to post volunteer sheets for each possible play activity, and allow a few pupils at a time to sign up for what they choose to participate in. If the acting list is too long, you may want to have two casts and two performances. It helps to have a stand-in in case of a performer's absence. If too many pupils want to write the play, divide them in two small writing groups to write two plays — one for performance later in the year. In the unlikely case that no one wants to write the play, you can probably get a few volunteers by suggesting that someone rewrite an old folk tale in his own words. This will give pupil left on the winning team. Another way is to declare the the confidence to start on the project. Another way is to offer to help, and to gradually withdraw from the writing group as they begin to get going.

Allow small groups to meet to write, to plan the production, to rehearse and to work on sets and costumes. You may be able to give children learning opportunities in mathematics, art and working with tools as they construct play sets. Fabrics, sewing and history may have to be studied in order to make appropriate costumes. The play's director will need to make a study of other plays and directing techniques so that he can direct well. The actors will benefit from tape recording their rehearsals and listening to themselves. They should also learn how to project their voices and improve their diction. The writers will be stimulated by reading books on how to write plays and by reading some of the great plays. If young children are involved, choose some suitable plays that they will enjoy reading.

So, the opportunities for research, creativity and learning are boundless in an activity such as this. Students of any age will grow from this type of experience while they have a marvelous time.

Spelldowns

A spelldown will never lose its appeal. It combines all of the excitement of a game with the practice and reinforcement of a good spelling lesson. You can make the spelldown much more valuable by having the pupils write the words on the board as well as spell them orally. Erase incorrect spellings as soon as you can, leaving only the correctly spelled words for the class to see.

One good way to conduct a spelldown is to divide the group into two equal teams standing on opposite sides of the room. The first member in line on one side will hear the word pronounced, repeated in a sentence and pronounced again. Then he will spell the word aloud and write it on the board or overhead projector, or just write it. The signal that a pupil has finished spelling his word can be his setting down the chalk. If the word is judged to be spelled correctly, he waits till everyone sees it, erases it and goes to the back of the line. Then the first one in line on the opposite team gets his turn to spell a new word.

If the word is spelled incorrectly, the teacher says, "Sorry — incorrect," and the pupil erases it quickly and sits down in his seat. The first one in the opposite team tries the same word. The second player to try the same word has the advantage of seeing which way is incorrect. This procedure should keep everyone watching closely, and the process continues until the word is spelled correctly.

The traditional spelldown continues until there is only one pupil left on the winning teams. Another way is to declare the first team to go below three members as the loser. These games are very time-consuming, so an even better way is to have the spelldown end at a set time, when the winning team will be the one with the most members.

I, personally, prefer not to have pupils eliminated and out of the game. They have less embarrassment and more practice if they stay in. In this way of playing, points can be given to teams for each correctly-spelled word. Then the winning team is the one with the most points at a set time.

Expect strict silence, and impose penalties (points lost, privileges taken away etc.) for any type of signal that will help a team member. You'll be surprised at how quiet they can be. Allow a reasonable time for each child to write his word, but if you allow too long a time, the game becomes tedious and loses its excitement.

Stained Glass Windows

Making imitation stained glass windows is an art activity that I still remember from my childhood because it was so enjoyable. It can be creative and very satisfying as children draw designs, cut them out and fill them in with colored transparent paper. The completed paper stained glass windows are very effective when attached to glass windows. This project will be done most effectively by upper grade children.

Begin with a sheet of colored construction paper for each child or for each two children. You may prefer to have two pupils work together on each "window," because it can become too time-consuming when done individually.

Show large color pictures of stained glass windows before the children begin work. Compare the leaded outlines with the construction paper frame, and relate the stained glass to the colored transparent paper that will be glued to the frame.

Remind children to use double lines at least one-fourth inch apart when they work on the construction paper frame design, so that there will be a sturdy frame left when they cut away the design.

Figure 5-4

The first step in the project is to draw a simple design. It can be based on curves, squares, rectangles, triangles or anything that the pupil wishes to draw.

After the design is set, the extra line to make it a frame can be added.

In most cases, sharp scissors will be adequate for cutting out the frame design and leaving spaces to be filled in with transparent paper. However, for small, intricate designs, have a few wooden cutting boards and razor blades *in holders.* The students can take turns using these under your supervision.

When the frames are ready, children can select their colors and plan how to fill in the spaces with transparent paper. It can be cut to approximate size for each design part and trimmed as they work.

The transparent paper must be glued from the back, so that the raw edges cannot be seen. Neatness and attention to detail are important in this activity.

Children will learn to share equipment and take turns as they work in pairs. Hopefully, they will also grow in understanding of each other's mistakes, as many will certainly be made.

If possible, select partners who will be compatible, and be on the watch for unequal distribution of work. If a child does not do his share it is better to switch him to another activity. This project can only be valuable to those who take pride in their creations and who put effort into them.

Finishing Tapes

A marvelous way to stimulate creativity in primary pupils is to have them finish a tape-recorded story that has been begun for them. This is especially beneficial for slower individuals who find it difficult, or impossible, to tackle an entire story on their own.

The best way to do this is to have one of your better oral readers tape record most of a story, leaving it unfinished. Then, some of your slower pupils can take turns listening to the story a few times. After that, provide them with paper and pencils and ask them to write their own endings. Encourage pupils to listen to the story again, as many times as they wish, so that they can see how their endings fit the story beginning.

In case you have a very slow child who needs to be encouraged in creative expression, allow this pupil to tape record his ending rather than write it out. He will probably be delighted with his own story ending.

Then, to provide him or her with writing practice, have the pupil listen to his own recorded ending and write it down. It will take more than one listening to accomplish this — it may take many — but the child will benefit a great deal from writing down his own story ending.

Recording

The former activity will lead naturally into this one. Children, being imitative and jealous of others, will all want to tape record stories once they see others have the opportunity to do it for parts of stories.

Although you need a well-read story to be effective for story-ending use, you can still use other sections of the tape just for this type of oral reading practice.

This recording is an activity that can be done by individuals in their spare time. Show them where to record on the tape, and ask them to give their names before they begin. Encourage pupils to first silently read through the story at least once, in order to become familiar with it and read it better.

Later, you can listen to the tape for diagnostic and grading purposes, and you will save the classroom time that would otherwise be spent listening to individuals do oral reading.

Metric Mysteries*

In this practice activity pupils will use clues to solve story puzzles and problems about the metric system. Points will be given for correctly solving them, with the number of points rising proportionately to the problems' difficulty.

Use the puzzles that apply to the metric system units that your students have already learned. Type each problem separately, with a self-checking slip to be given out when each puzzle is completed. Pupils will check their answers and turn in the marked problems to you on a daily or weekly basis. Add similar problems so that you can have regular independent practice work on a large variety of them.

After checking the marked puzzles, keep a record of the points earned. The daily or weekly winner of the most points can have his or her name written on a continuing posted chart headed by the title, "Metric Marvels."

The following charts will be useful in all of your work with the metric system:

UNIT	MILLIMETER	CENTIMETER	DECIMETER	METER
millimeter (mm)	1	1/10	1/100	1/1000
centimeter (cm)	10	1	1/10	1/100
decimeter (dm)	100	10	1	1/10
meter (m)	1000	100	10	1

Figure 5-5

*Rosalind Ashley

Decimal Numeration System	Thousands	Hundreds	Tens	Ones	Tenths	Hundredths	Thousandths
Place Name Metric Unit	Kilometer 1000 meters	Hectometer 100 meters	Dekameter 10 meters	METER (Basic Unit) 1 meter	Decimeter 1/10 meter	Centimeter 1/100 meter	Millimeter 1/1000 meter
Interre-lations, Metric Units of Length	100 dekameters 10 hectometers	10 dekameters				1/10 decimeter	1/100 decimeter 1/10 centimeter

Figure 5-6

METRIC PREFIXES

1/1000 = milli
1/100 = centi
1/10 = deci
10 = deka
100 = hecto
1000 = kilo

Figure 5-7

You may wish to post copies of these charts on the bulletin board so that students can refer to them as they solve the puzzles. The *Metric Mysteries* that follow are ready to use.

CLUES: 1 km = 0.621 mi.
          1 mi. = 1.609 km

MYSTERY: My school is one kilometer away from my house. But, all the road signs are given in miles. About how far away is it in miles?
a) 1-1/2 miles
b) 1 mile
c) 6/10 mile
d) 1/10 mile

POINTS: 1   ANSWER: c) about 6/10 mile

CLUES: 10 dm = 1 m
          100 cm = 1 m
          1000 mm = 1 m

MYSTERY: John was discussing the metric system with a friend, and he said, "The word 'millimeter' tells you exactly what it is." What did he mean?

POINTS: 1   ANSWER: "Milli" means one thousandth.
                         A <u>millimeter</u> is one thousandth of a meter.

CLUES: 1 dm is about 4 in.
         1 m is about 3-3/8 in. longer than a yd.
         1 m is about 39 in.

MYSTERY: The customary unit of measurement closest to the meter is a:
         a) rod
         b) foot
         c) inch
         d) yard

POINTS: 1   ANSWER: d) yard

CLUES: 1 meter = 1000 millimeters
         1 kilometer = 0.621 mile
         1 meter = 1.093 yard

MYSTERY: What would be the <u>best</u> unit to use to measure a tall person?
         a) kilometer
         b) meter
         c) millimeter
         d) hectometer

POINTS: 2   ANSWER: b) meter

CLUES: 1 dm = 10 cm
         1 cm = 10 mm

MYSTERY: My teacher wants me to give an answer in millimeters. I have a line that's 14 cm long. How long is it?

POINTS: 2   ANSWER: 140 mm (Multiply by 10.)

CLUES: 1 kilometer is a little over half a mile.
         1 meter equals 1000 millimeters.
         1 liter is a little more than 1 quart.
         1 meter is about 39 inches.

MYSTERY: My dad is using wrenches to work on small things in his foreign car. What unit would he probably use in measuring?
  a) meters
  b) liters
  c) millimeters
  d) kilometers

POINTS: 3   ANSWER: c) millimeters

CLUES: 1 m = 100 cm
          1 cm = 10 mm

MYSTERY: Our car is about how long?
  a) 5 m
  b) 15 mm
  c) 26 m
  d) 3 cm

POINTS: 3   ANSWER: a) 5 m

CLUES: A penny weighs about 3 grams.
          A nickel weighs about 5 grams.
          It takes almost 28-1/2 grams to make 1 ounce.

MYSTERY: I have eight pennies and one nickel. My sister says that all together they weigh more than 1 ounce. I say that they weigh less. Who's correct?

POINTS: 3   ANSWER: Your sister. They weigh about 29 grams. There are less than 28-1/2 grams in 1 ounce.

CLUES: 100 cm = 1 m   1 mi. = 1.609 km
          1 m = 1.093 yd.   1 km = 0.621 mi.
          1 liter is a little more than 1/4 gal.

MYSTERY: We were very tired from our five mile walk. About how far did we go?
  a) 8 centimeters
  b) 8 liters
  c) 8 meters
  d) 8 kilometers

POINTS: 4   ANSWER: d) 8 kilometers

CLUES: 4 quarts = 1 gallon
1/4 gallon = a little less than 1 liter
2 pints = a little less than 1 liter

MYSTERY: I have a liter full of orange juice. I have four containers
and I can't figure out which one to use. Which one is
closest to a liter in capacity?
a) a gallon
b) a pint
c) a quart
d) a cup

POINTS: 4   ANSWER: c) Use the quart container and
drink the little bit that's left.

CLUES: 1 cm = 10 mm
1 dm = 10 cm

MYSTERY: How many mm are there in 6-1/2 cm?

POINTS: 5   ANSWER: 65 mm (Multiply by 10.)

CLUES: 1 dm = 10 cm
1 dm = 100 mm

MYSTERY: We had to decide which one of the following was the
greatest. What do you think?
a) 456 mm
b) 52 cm
c) 4.6 dm
d) 52 mm

POINTS: 5   ANSWER: b) 52 cm

CLUES: 1 m = 10 dm
1 m = 1000 mm

MYSTERY: Then we had to decide which one of the following was
the smallest. What do you think?
a) 62 dm
b) 8 m
c) 742 mm
d) 2 km

POINTS: 5   ANSWER: c) 742 mm

CLUES: 1 cm = 1/10 dm
            10 cm = 1 dm
            1 dm is about 4 in.

MYSTERY: How many centimeters are about the same length as
                 2 inches?
                 a) 3 cm
                 b) 4 cm
                 c) 5 cm
                 d) 2/5 cm

POINTS: 5   ANSWER: c) 5 cm

CLUES: 1 dm = 10 cm
            1 m = 100 cm
            1 m = 10 dm
            1 dm = about 4 in.

MYSTERY: Which one of the following statements is <u>not</u> true?
                 a) 2 ft. is shorter than 6 dm + 2 cm.
                 b) 1 yd. is longer than 8 dm.
                 c) 29 cm = 2 dm + 9 cm
                 d) 347 dm = 3 m + 4 dm + 7 cm

POINTS: 6   ANSWER: d) 347 dm = 3 m + 4 dm
                             + 7 cm

CLUES: 1 dm = 1/10 m   1 dm = 10 cm
            1 cm = 1/100 m   1 dm = 100 mm
            1 mm = 1/1000 m

MYSTERY: Choose the one <u>correct</u> statement from the incorrect
                ones:
                 a) 4 cm = 40 dm
                 b) 3 dm + 2 cm = 32 cm
                 c) 3 m = 20 dm + 100 mm
                 d) 44 cm = 4 m + 4 cm

POINTS: 6   ANSWER: b) 3 dm + 2 cm = 32 cm

CLUES: 1 cm = 1/100 m
            1 dm = 1/10 m
            1000 m = 1 km

MYSTERY: Which one of the following is <u>incorrect</u>?
                 a) 1.35 m = 135 cm

        b) 2500 m $=$ 2.5 km
        c) 250 cm $=$ 25 m
        d) 750 dm $=$ 75 m

POINTS: 6   ANSWER: c) 250 cm $=$ 25 m

CLUES: 1 kilogram is about 2-1/5 pounds.
           1000 grams $=$ 1 kilogram

MYSTERY: Betty weighs 20,000 grams, my sister Carrie weighs
            60 pounds and Joan weighs 30 kilograms. Choose the
            answer that shows the girls' names in order, going
            from the heaviest to the lightest in weight.
            a) Joan, Carrie, Betty
            b) Carrie, Joan, Betty
            c) Betty, Joan, Carrie
            d) Joan, Betty, Carrie

POINTS: 7   ANSWER: a) Joan, 66 pounds; Carrie, 60
                               pounds; Betty, 44 pounds.

You will find the series called *Working With Color Rods in Metric Measurement** very useful. These books contain NTC Duplicating Masters that teach, and give practice in, the metric system.

Units I, II and III introduce the metric units *millimeter, centimeter, decimeter, meter, square millimeter, square centimeter, square decimeter, square meter, cubic centimeter, cubic decimeter* and *liter.*

Pupils learn how to measure, find the area, find volume, record and convert from one of these units to another, beginning with physical models which students can see, touch and manipulate. There are also lessons on decimals.

A good article about metric teaching activities and metric workshops is "Don't Just Think Metric — Live Metric."†

---

*Joseph P. Cech and Carl Seltzer, *Working With Color Rods in Metric Measurement,* Unit I, *Metric Length;* Unit II, *Metric Area;* Unit III, *Metric Volume* (Skokie, Ill.: National Textbook Co., 1974).

† Richard J. Shumway and Larry Sachs, "Don't Just Think Metric — Live Metric," *The Arithmetic Teacher,* Vol. 22, No. 2, Feb., 1975, 103-10.

Beginner's Metric Poster Cards, Copyright 1973 by Milton Bradley Company

Figure 5-8

Another helpful article and test for teachers on the metric system is "Mathematics — A Metric Test For You."[*]

Beginner's Metric System Poster Cards[†]

This new set contains six, full-color picture story poster cards that introduce comparative aspects of the metric and English systems to measure weight, volume and distance. Three meter-yard comparison charts are also included for large measurements. The reverse sides of posters contain extended activities to improve familiarity with the metric system, and a teacher's guide offers detailed explanations. These poster cards will be very useful in teaching this system, which can be difficult for some students.

Composing a Song

If you are fortunate enough to know music, you can do this project on your own. However, even if you don't, you can enlist the aid of a special music teacher or a capable student with musical training. Be willing to admit that you don't know something, because it makes children want to help and want to learn even more.

A piano is a must for this activity, so in case you cannot move one into your classroom, reserve the music room or the auditorium for a few periods and bring in a portable chalkboard for the lesson.

Touching and Writing

It can be very interesting and educational to provide a variety of objects for children to touch and write about.

Set up a display table with a group of objects that have distinctive tactile qualities. For example: velvet, sandpaper, a piece of carpeting, a peeled ear of corn, satin, a rough rock, corduroy etc.

Have children go up to the table in pairs, taking turns with one child in each pair blindfolded. As soon as each blindfolded

---

[*]Richard Bowles, "Mathematics — A Metric Test For You," *Instructor*, Vol. LXXXIV, No. 6, Feb., 1975, 59-61.

[†] Beginner's Metric Poster Cards, Copyright 1973 by Milton Bradley Company. Reproduced with permission of Milton Bradley Company, Springfield, Mass. 01101.

pupil returns to his desk, ask him to write about one or more of the objects that he has just touched.

The sense of touch will stimulate the child's imagination, and it may lead him beyond simple guessing about the objects. One pupil wrote a very interesting paragraph about petting his cat. He was reminded of the tactile sensations of stroking the cat when he touched the velvet fabric.

You can set up different objects so that the other pupil in each pair will get a turn too. At that time his partner will be leading him up to the table to touch the objects.

This activity can be good writing practice, an extension of awareness of the tactile sense and also a great deal of fun as children go to the display table afterwards and try to identify what they had previously been guessing at.

HOW TO INDIVIDUALIZE WITH BULLETIN BOARD PROJECTS

Consider bulletin boards as learning and helping opportunities for your pupils. Pupil bulletin board projects can also be very enjoyable for them to work on.

If you select children's tasks carefully they are strictly educational, as well as helpful; and we all know that the teacher's work is endless. Share the routine tasks of the project among all the students, as they have a need to be useful. All pupils crave to help their teacher, and they gain in self esteem if they are allowed to do this and if they complete it successfully.

Expect pupils to do some thinking and to create their own displays. Children must not be used to staple up *your* ideas except for occasional help. Be on hand to provide materials and encouragement, but challenge youngsters to think of ideas and ways to carry them out. Demand effort on their part, but be very uncritical of their results and of their neatness. You can be proud of the board no matter what it looks like, if it has been a real learning experience for your pupils.

Most of your bulletin board displays will come from children's suggestions as a direct result of your units of study in various subjects. Displays of student work are also good for bulletin boards, and these can be made original and artistic by group effort and discussion of ideas.

Each child has some talent or interest that you can use in a bulletin board project. Give art work to those who excel in art, research work to those who do it well and planning and responsibility to pupils who are capable.

However, within the limits of their abilities, try to vary the tasks so that children will have opportunities for *new* experiences too. Give responsibility to those who may grow as a result of it, and encourage creativity in pupils who may never have displayed a trace of it. Experiences such as bulletin board projects are so open-ended that they can develop creativity and talent that you and the pupils were unaware of until then.

SAMPLE GAME — CAMERA SAFARI

This original ready-to-use social studies board game about a camera safari in Africa is suitable for students in the sixth through eighth grades. The players (two through five) can be represented as they travel on the board by buttons or small cardboard pictures of people. The board diagram can be drawn on a *large* sheet of paper, allowing enough space for the writing in the boxes.

Players begin their safari in the START box on the board, and they move toward the FINISH box on instructions from a deck of cards, which they draw and read aloud in turn. All players start the game with fifty slips of paper, each of which represents a roll of unexposed film.

The following instructions on some of the seventy-five boxes on the safari board tell players what to do with their film. The paper that represents film is folded and kept by the player to signify when it is used, or exposed. If a player lands on a box that tells him that film is lost or damaged, the appropriate kind of film is turned in to film bank. If exposed film is demanded and the player has none, unexposed film is turned in. The winner of the game is the player with the most rolls of exposed film when the game ends.

To construct the game, copy the diagram shown in Figure 5-9. It should have seventy-five large boxes, including the START and FINISH boxes.

Give each player fifty slips of paper, and plan on enough for five students.

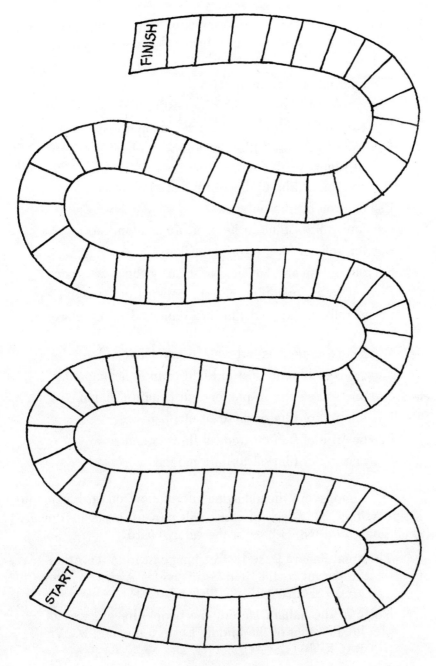

Figure 5-9

At intervals on the board, use manuscript writing to copy the following player instructions in some of the boxes. All film is unexposed unless instructions say otherwise.

Use one roll of film on giraffes.

Three rolls of film are taken by hostile natives.

Use two rolls of film on village ceremonial dancers.

Four rolls of exposed film are lost when boat overturns in Congo River.

Use one roll of film on beautiful waterfall and rapids.

Use one roll of film on apes.

Use four rolls of film on herd of hippopotamuses.

Use ten rolls of film on pride of lions.

Six rolls of film are damaged in security check at airport.

Five rolls of exposed film are lost escaping from crocodiles.

Seven rolls of exposed film are damaged by excessive heat.

You meet a camera expert who gives you five rolls of film.

Four rolls of film are lost in flight from attacking ants.

Use one roll of film to photograph beautiful impala.

Use one roll of film on herd of elephants.

Use one roll of film on tropical flowers and ferns.

Use one roll of film on termite mound.

Have pupils copy the following information* on cards in manuscript writing. This deck of cards will move the players toward their goal, the FINISH box on the safari board.

The great Sahara Desert, stretching east from the Atlantic Ocean to the Red Sea, divides Africa in two. MOVE FORWARD THREE SPACES.

North of the Sahara Desert, the people have a way of life like that of the Middle Eastern peoples. MOVE BACK TWO SPACES.

---

*Melvin Schwartz and John R. O'Connor, *Exploring Africa South of the Sahara* (New York: Globe Book Co., Inc., 1973).

South of the Sahara Desert, the people are largely blacks whose ways of living are different from their northern neighbors. MOVE FORWARD ONE SPACE.

Africa is separated from Europe by the Mediterranean Sea. MOVE FORWARD SIX SPACES.

To the west of Africa is the Atlantic Ocean. MOVE FORWARD FOUR SPACES.

To the east of Africa (south of the Gulf of Aden) is the Indian Ocean. MOVE BACK THREE SPACES.

Africa's geography makes it into two different regions. MOVE FORWARD ONE SPACE.

Africa is a giant continent eleven million square miles in area. MOVE FORWARD SEVEN SPACES.

Africa is larger than either North or South America. MOVE BACK TWO SPACES.

Africa is three times the size of the United States. MOVE FORWARD NINE SPACES.

Africa lies south of the continent of Europe. MOVE BACK THREE SPACES.

The African nations south of the Sahara have been free only a short time. MOVE FORWARD TWO SPACES.

Africa south of the Sahara is rich in mineral resources such as gold, diamonds, uranium, copper, bauxite and manganese. MOVE FORWARD THREE SPACES.

The African nations now have more votes than any other group in the United Nations General Assembly. MOVE FORWARD ONE SPACE.

Some of the African nations south of the Sahara have had trouble setting up strong and lasting governments. MOVE BACK TWO SPACES.

Some railroad workers in South Africa earn less than one hundred dollars a year. MOVE BACK FOUR SPACES.

Many black Americans call themselves Afro-Americans to recall the fact that their ancestors, first homeland was the continent of Africa. MOVE FORWARD THREE SPACES.

Less than fifty years ago, Africa had few nations, but the new nations today are called "emerging" or "developing" countries. MOVE FORWARD TWELVE SPACES.

Most of Africa is a plateau. MOVE BACK EIGHT SPACES.

Africa has very little coastal lowland, and the land rises sharply near the coast and slopes down toward the center like a saucer. MOVE FORWARD NINE SPACES.

The plateaus (large areas of level highlands) of Africa below the Sahara are drained by three large rivers: the Congo, Zambezi and Niger. MOVE FORWARD THREE SPACES.

The African rivers south of the Sahara begin on high ground and flow rapidly down to the narrow coastal plains with rapids and falls. MOVE BACK ONE SPACE.

Mount Kilimanjaro and Mount Kenya, on Africa's east coast, are almost on the equator, yet they are so high that they are covered with ice and snow. MOVE FORWARD TWO SPACES.

Snow from the mountains has provided water for huge lakes in the valleys of the African highlands: Lake Victoria, Lake Tanganyika and Lake Nyasa. MOVE FORWARD TEN SPACES.

The Sahara Desert makes it hard to reach central Africa by land from the North. MOVE FORWARD FOUR SPACES.

The African coastline has few good harbors. MOVE BACK TWO SPACES.

Many of Africa's river mouths are hard to enter because of deltas and sandbars. MOVE FORWARD FOUR SPACES.

Transportation up the rivers is not easy because of falls and rapids. MOVE BACK FIVE SPACES.

African tribes are often unfriendly to strangers because many Africans were taken as slaves in the past. MOVE FORWARD TWO SPACES.

The equator runs through the middle of Africa. MOVE BACK TWO SPACES.

Africa south of the Sahara has a hot climate. MOVE FORWARD TEN SPACES.

Africa has a large rain forest on the equator. MOVE FORWARD TWO SPACES.

Trees and plants grow very close together in Africa's rain forest. MOVE FORWARD ONE SPACE.

Many kinds of birds, snakes, monkeys and apes live in Africa's rain forest. MOVE BACK TWO SPACES.

The rain forest of Africa is full of mosquitoes that carry malaria and yellow fever. MOVE BACK TWO SPACES.

The tsetse (TSET see) fly of Africa carries deadly sleeping sickness. MOVE FORWARD THREE SPACES.

Most of tropical Africa is not a rain forest, but a hot grassland called a savanna. MOVE BACK FOUR SPACES.

The African savannas (or grasslands) lie north and south of the rain forest. MOVE BACK TWO SPACES.

Most of Africa's large animals — the antelope, lion, elephant, giraffe and zebra live on the savannas (grasslands). MOVE FORWARD TWO SPACES.

North and south of the African savannas (grasslands) are the deserts. MOVE BACK FOUR SPACES.

The great Sahara Desert takes up nearly all of the northern part of Africa. MOVE BACK TWO SPACES.

The Kalahari Desert, in southern Africa, is smaller than the Sahara, yet it is as large as all of Western Europe. MOVE FORWARD SIX SPACES.

Many of the African governments have set aside land

called preserves to protect wild animals from hunters. MOVE FORWARD FIVE SPACES.

Most people in Africa are farmers and raise food chiefly
for their own use. MOVE FORWARD FOUR
SPACES.

It is very difficult to travel in Africa because of the
thick forests, deserts, mountains and dangerous
rivers. MOVE BACK TWO SPACES.

It is now believed that the first human life on earth began in Africa with hunters and gatherers of food.
MOVE BACK ONE SPACE.

The first great farming civilization in Africa began along
the Nile River in Egypt. MOVE FORWARD SEVEN
SPACES.

The land along the Nile River has fertile soil for growing
crops because the river overflows its banks each
year. MOVE BACK TWO SPACES.

Moslem traders from North Africa travel across the
desert to reach the black people of South Africa.
MOVE FORWARD NINE SPACES.

Sailors from Asia brought two new crops to Africa which
grew well in the hot, wet forests: bananas and yams.
MOVE FORWARD THREE SPACES.

In the seventh century, a new religion, called Islam,
started in Arabia. The Moslems (people who followed this religion) carried the religion across the
Sahara Desert. MOVE BACK FOUR SPACES.

The kingdom of Ghana, in west Africa, is the oldest of
the new African republics. It was very powerful
long ago because its people used iron, which made
them stronger than their neighbors. MOVE FOR-
WARD ONE SPACE.

Africa was held back in its development because the
difficulty of travel kept tribes apart, there was
constant warfare and short life spans because of
illness. MOVE BACK TWO SPACES.

African tribes made slaves of their prisoners long before the coming of Europeans. MOVE FORWARD THREE SPACES.

In the 1500's Europeans bought slaves at African coastal ports from strong Negro tribes who raided other villages. MOVE FORWARD THREE SPACES.

European slave traders, while waiting for slaves, planted New World crops such as corn, peanuts, tobacco, potatoes and tomatoes. These crops were later planted by African farmers. MOVE BACK TWO SPACES.

Many missionaries such as Dr. Livingstone, came to Africa to help the people and to teach them the Christian religion. MOVE FORWARD ONE SPACE.

Some famous explorers of Africa in the nineteenth century were Mungo Park, John Speke, Samuel Baker, Dr. David Livingstone and Henry Stanley. MOVE BACK TWO SPACES.

When word of Africa's riches — gold, ivory, animal skins and fine woods — reached Europe in the nineteenth century, Africa was soon colonized and divided up by the nations of western Europe. MOVE FORWARD TWO SPACES.

Much of South Africa remained under European control until after World War II, when African peoples won their freedom. MOVE FORWARD SEVEN SPACES.

Because African independent nations are composed of many, many tribes, each with its own language and rulers, it causes a problem for the new governments. MOVE BACK ONE SPACE.

Some Africans raise cattle and some grow manioc, plantains and rice. Others catch fish and collect coconuts. MOVE FORWARD THREE SPACES.

Cacao (for chocolate), coffee, palm nuts, and rubber are important African crops. MOVE FORWARD NINE SPACES.

Mahogany and ebony are valuable rain forest trees, but it is difficult to get the wood to the seaports. MOVE BACK FOUR SPACES.

CHANCE CARDS

Stop at city to hire a new guide. MISS ONE TURN.

Arrive at impassable river. GO BACK EIGHT SPACES.

Stop at friendly village to hire two men for safari. MOVE FORWARD ONE SPACE.

Stop when narrow path is blocked by underbrush. STOP FOR ONE TURN TO CLEAR PATH.

Go back for Land Rover repairs. MISS ONE TURN.

CHECKLIST

* Use games and game-like activities to give pupils stimulation, enjoyment and information.
* Allow students to help in the research and construction of games.
* Get game ideas from Material Centers, books, catalogs, libraries, university curriculum centers and other teachers.
* Use simulations for the understanding and insights they give.
* Stimulate writing creativity with comic strip stories.
* Motivate children to create, produce and act in their own plays.
* Enjoy spelldowns for practice, and present the correctly spelled words visually.
* Create imitation stained glass windows for a satisfying art activity.
* Have pupils finish tape-recorded story beginnings.
* Encourage oral reading by allowing pupils to use a tape recorder.
* Teach the metric system with colorful posters and many practice activities.
* Have the class compose a song, using the help of a music teacher or a capable student, if necessary.
* Provide tactile experiences to stimulate pupils' imagination and senses.
* Make use of bulletin boards as learning and creativity experiences for students.
* Delegate some bulletin boards regularly to different capable pupils, and expect them to plan and carry them out on their own.

6

Developing Individual Interests with Optional Groupings

There is something about choosing one's own learning activity that changes a pupil's entire attitude. All of a sudden he is in charge of what he's doing, and it becomes important to him. Some children become frustrated in making their own choices and should not be required to do so. However, most pupils get a great deal of motivation from choosing some of their activities.

Even when his choice is between two activities that the pupil knows nothing about and has no particular interest in, the option generates a feeling of caring, and an interest can develop if it is at all possible. Since there are so many worthwhile learning projects that a child has never had the opportunity to explore, the chance to choose what he is going to do can expose him to something that can become a real interest in the future.

Once a pupil's choice is made, he is expected to give it a chance for at least one session. If the optional activity proves to be of no interest to the child, he is free not to continue with it for any more lessons.

You will find that after a while pupils will be suggesting optional activities to you, as well as requesting repeats of former projects. In this way, the children become self-starters in the truest sense. They not only have the enthusiasm to begin a new project — they plan and create their own projects. It can become the most satisfying and productive kind of learning.

This chapter shows you how to start and get the most out of interclass special interest groups, how to plan optional groupings in a self-contained classroom, how to use clubs to individualize; and it also provides an Interest Inventory for older students. It answers the question, "Does the teacher have to join all the clubs?" It offers suggestions on first aid for ailing clubs and it discusses interclub projects. It also tells you how to avoid having an elite group.

INTERCLASS SPECIAL INTEREST GROUPS

A wonderful way to add some zest to your teaching, especially mid-year, is to arrange with two other teachers for a free hour about twice a week for all the children in the three classes to pursue a special interest.

For example, one teacher may have a group that is making its own large map of the United States from a map projected on a wall. A large sheet of paper can be taped to the wall. The children may work on it for three or four sessions, tracing the map, filling in the names of states, state capitols, and important lakes and rivers and coloring it with colored chalk. Each state would be colored a different color than the nearby states. A great deal of geographical learning can happen as children consult an atlas for details, and argue endlessly over the location and shapes of various states, cities, rivers and lakes.

Another teacher may have a special art project that children can sign up for such as a collage; or making decorated vases with glued-on macaroni and spraying them with gold paint.

A third teacher might have a science project in which the students make slides and use microscopes. Her group could collect specimens to examine.

Before the projects begin, each teacher posts sign-up sheets in her class for all three special interest groups. When the agreed-on total number of pupils have signed up, the class is closed. If there is a big demand for the special project, pupils can be encouraged to sign up for the preferred project when it begins again in a few weeks. There will probably be an uneven number of pupils in each of the three groups, but when the class limit is reached, pupils will have to sign up for the remaining projects or elect to read library books. No pupil is ever forced to join one of the groups. In the unlikely case that only a few, or no pupils sign up for a project, it is, of course, dropped and another chosen to take its place.

In this way, most pupils get to participate in a special interest group that may be totally unconnected with their daily work, that is educational as well as fun. It's a great way to broaden children's interests.

This project can be done well with two classes as well as three, but the opportunities for special ideas, talents and variety in the optional offerings is even greater with three teachers.

There could be an endless list of special projects ranging from writing haiku, listening to classical music, creative dramatics and sketching, to reading and discussing biographies. Anything that the teachers want to do would be good, and if the children really like it very much, it would naturally be continued for the others to try too. Aim for a balance in the activities, as the group should not always do art projects, or work in any other subject area all of the time.

The enthusiasm started by this type of interclass project will carry through the rest of the school day. Everyone learns from the projects and enjoys them. Another benefit is the opportunity to interact with other teachers and with students from other classes.

PLANNING OPTIONAL GROUPINGS IN A
SELF-CONTAINED CLASSROOM

It is not necessary to join forces with two other teachers and classes in order to have optional groupings for special interests. This type of free self-chosen activity can also be handled in a self-contained classroom by one teacher.

However, the planning for this must be done in a slightly different way than for the interclass special interest groups. If you have a student teacher or a teacher aide, it will work almost as easily, and if there is a nearby place where the other group can work, there will be no distractions from noise or curiosity. But, if you are alone, you will probably want to schedule only one special group at a time, while the rest of the class does a writing, mathematics, spelling practice or reading assignment.

Simultaneous Poetry and Figure Drawing Projects

It is possible to have two special interest groups during the same class session if you can plan different times for when they will need you. For example, schedule the following two optional groupings:

Creative writing — poetry

Art — figure drawing

All that you need to do is to alternate between the groups. It isn't easy, but it can be done well if you plan ahead. Give the creative writing people some exceptionally good poems of different types to read. For instance, provide ahead of time a variety of poems which could include limericks, haiku and some different famous poems.

Any suitable poetry books will do for the beginning reading and motivational time, if you have enough copies that include the poems you have chosen. Or, you may wish to duplicate the poems you select. Do not just give the pupils a poetry book and tell them to read poems. They'll lose interest right away, unless you choose suitable poems that they will understand and enjoy. There are many fine poems that you can select. Avoid those with elaborate symbolism and difficult language that need a lot of explanation, even for older students. A fine book of poetry for young pupils is *The World's So Big.** Excellent poems for mature students can be found in *Sound and Sense: An Introduction to Poetry.*†

Of course, the level of the poetry will vary with the age and reading ability of your students. Young pupils will enjoy "Mud" by Polly Chase Boyden, "Something to Think About" by Rowena Bennett, "The Storm" by Dorothy Aldis and "Drinking Fountain" by Marchette Chute, all of which can be found in *The World's So Big.* Advanced eighth graders and older students would understand and enjoy much in the following: Robert Frost's "Stopping by Woods on a Snowy Evening," e. e. cummings' "in Just —," Ogden Nash's "The Turtle," Carl Sandburg's "Fog," Edgar Allan Poe's "Annabel Lee," Walt Whitman's "O Captain! My Captain! " Alfred Noyes' "The Highwayman" and Alfred, Lord Tennyson's "The Eagle." Many poems, such as "in Just —"‡ and "Stopping by Woods

---

*Charlotte S. Huck, William A. Jenkins, and Wilma J. Pyle (compiled by), *The World's So Big* (Glenview, Ill.: Scott, Foresman and Co.), 1971. Scott Foresman Reading Systems, Level 2, Teacher's Read-Aloud Library.

† Laurence Perrine, *Sound and Sense: An Introduction to Poetry* (New York: Harcourt, Brace and Co.), 1956.

‡ Mr. Cummings has recorded "in Just—" (78 rpm, Linguaphone Institute, HBC).

on a Snowy Evening"* have been recorded by the poets themselves. Your group may enjoy listening to these recordings. While your poetry people are reading or listening to this rich variety, join the artists, give out art paper and charcoal, select a model, help the model get set in a comfortable pose and have the art group start working. Provide extra paper for second and third attempts, and encourage them to draw their own *impressions* of the figure in case they are worried about their figure drawing ability.

Return to the poetry group, provide lined paper and pencils, and have a *short* discussion about the many styles of poetry. Try to bring out these points in the discussion: the intensity of language, the deepening and communication of important experience, the appeal to the senses, the emotion and the imagination. Mention that poetry may be beautiful, ugly, sad or humorous. Be sure to encourage students to select their own style of writing, and emphasize that rhyme or form is not important.

While the poetry group is trying to write poems, return to the figure drawing group and give the model a rest period. Visit each student and try to give some helpful comment or encouragement on his work. Since practice and encouragement are the two best ways to improve in figure drawing, avoid any criticism. In case you have someone who is too discouraged to wish to continue, provide a still life display for him to draw from. It is better to encourage a successful experience with a different kind of model than to have the student just give up and believe that he can't draw.

Do not select a drawing as the best, to hold up for the others, to admire, as it may inhibit or discourage their own efforts. The successful student has the reward of his good drawing and he doesn't need any more, because he can see that it's good. If you wish to display the art, plan on displaying all of it. Certain pupils will request that you not put up their work, and if you're sure that they mean it, you can respect their wishes. In this way, competition will be played down and no one will have the embarrassment of having his work rejected for display.

Start the model in his pose again, and go back to the poetry group. Read the beginning creative efforts with the same type

---

* Mr. Frost has recorded "Stopping by Woods on a Snowy Evening" (78 rpm, National Council of Teachers of English, RS70-1; or LP, National Council of Teachers of English, RL20-1).

of encouragement and helpful suggestions that you used with the artists. If the poem is bad, the student will usually know it anyway, so he doesn't need any more discouragement.

If a student is copying a theme, but using original language, allow him to continue without commenting on the copying. If the poem is an almost direct copy of one he's read, discuss new ideas with him based on his own experiences. Encourage him to use a thesaurus and a dictionary to get new words to enrich the imagery of his poem. Suggest a short two or three line poem that describes something he considers important, or very beautiful or ugly; or a feeling.

Be very accepting about all creative offerings, as it may take a while, and a few poor efforts, before a student can compose a truly satisfying poem. There will be a real happiness and excitement when the student creates something that he knows is good.

Pyramid and Sphinx Construction

Two interesting projects that could easily be done together are the study and construction of models of the Great Pyramid of Egypt and the Great Sphinx of Egypt.

Research would have to be done on each one to get the correct facts necessary to construct them. The construction would be of papier-mâché, clay or some other plastic material. The students would also be interested to find out the purposes for which the originals were built, and some of the difficulties involved in building them without machinery.

The children will enjoy reading or hearing the ancient myth about the sphinx, an imaginary creature. In the Greek myth, the sphinx was a wicked being with the body of a lion, the head of a woman, the wings of a bird and the tail of a serpent. This creature lived in a cliff just outside the city of Thebes, and it guarded the road that led to the city. The sphinx stopped every traveler and asked him this riddle: *What animal walks on four legs in the morning, two at noon and three in the evening?* If the traveler could not give the correct answer, the sphinx ate him immediately. When Oedipus passed by, the sphinx asked him the riddle. Oedipus answered that the animal in the riddle was man, because man walked on hands and feet when he was very young, on two feet when in the middle of life and with a staff when in old age. The sphinx was so angry because Oedipus had given the correct answer that she howled with rage; threw herself from the rocks and died.

The research groups can find a great deal of interesting materials, as well as drawings, about the Great Pyramids and the Great Sphinx from encyclopedias, textbooks and trade books about ancient Egypt.

A valuable extension from the Great Pyramid project can be a study of the pyramids of Mexico. A new special interest group may choose to study and construct a replica of the famous Pyramid of the Sun near Mexico City.

The students will find the history of these Mexican pyramids fascinating. They will also enjoy comparing the differences in shape between the famous Mexican and Egyptian pyramids.

Any of the activities suggested for interclass special interest groups would be suitable for the optional groupings in your own class. Use your special talents and interests, and the ideas of the children, to branch out into new projects that will enrich you as well as your pupils.

USING CLUBS TO INDIVIDUALIZE

The idea of optional groupings can be extended to continue developing a child's interest or talent in special interest clubs that meet regularly. The club or clubs can meet in a free enrichment time, during recess or before or after school. Clubs that require your special help or extra safety precautions should not meet during regular class time. You may wish to schedule a daily independent working time with a different club meeting each day.

Clubs can help to identify a pupil's talent as well as develop it. The child does not have to be bright in the traditionally accepted sense of being talented or "bright" in one special field. Each child is free to join, or drop out of, one or more clubs, strictly on the basis of his interest in the subject. Children who are interested or talented could enjoy a club in any subject area. Some possible types of clubs could be: stamps, mathematics, creative writing, plays, science, travel, singing, debating, cooking, model planes, mechanics, business, painting, ceramics, gardening, classical music, book discussions, figure drawing, creative writing, mystery stories etc.

The first step in individualizing instruction by using clubs is to identify a child's interests. Testing is only one way to identify a child's real interests. The following Interest Inventory will help you to identify older children's interests. It can be shortened and modified for use with younger pupils.

INTEREST INVENTORY

NAME _____ AGE _____

GRADE _____ SEX _____

What is your favorite hobby? _____
Any others? _____
When you have free time to do what you want, what do you like to do? _____
What game do you like best? _____
Any others? _____
Do you like to make things? _____
What do you like to make? _____
Do you like to do science experiments? _____
What kind? _____
Do you like to read? _____
What books have you enjoyed reading more than any others?

_____

What do you like to read about? Underline the names of these things and add others.

animals	science	mysteries	sports
biographies	funny things	science-fiction	politics
how-to-do-it books		adventure stories	

What person do you want to be like? (in real life or stories)

_____

What kind of work would you like to do some day? _____

_____

What sort of things do you do well? _____

_____

If you could have three wishes come true about yourself, what would they be?
1. _____
2. _____
3. _____

If you could have three wishes come true about school, what would they be?

1. _____

2. _____

3. _____

What are your favorite sports? _____

_____

What are your favorite subjects in school? _____

_____

Figure 6-1

You can get clues to a pupil's interests by observing what he reads and by listening to what he talks about and the questions he asks.

If you have club meetings on different days, this will encourage students to join more than one, and it may work out better by giving children a chance to try out different clubs. It will also give each club more members.

Once you have identified the students' major interests and have a fairly stable club membership in each field of interest, it will be more possible for you to work with individuals. In some cases you will be able to learn from them as they work on special projects with which you are unfamiliar. Showing his teacher something that is new to her can be an educational experience for a student, so don't be ashamed to admit that there's something you don't know.

The camaraderie and excitement of a club meeting in which a project is being planned and worked on can bring unlimited opportunities for communication with individuals. Your suggestions and help will be welcomed, and your enthusiasm will be enjoyed.

If no club project can be agreed on, or if nothing special is planned, postpone the meeting rather than have it unproductive. Have books ready that will provide ideas, inspiration and facts for each special interest club. The members may choose to spend an occasional meeting just browsing through the books looking for ideas. Use these times for individual conferences with club members, to give them help or encouragement about their interests. Individuals may just need someone who will listen to them while they describe a project, an experiment or a creation.

Does the Teacher Have to Join All the Clubs?

Yes. But we won't say *have* to. You'll *want* to, because you'll be so curious about what the children are doing.

Even if the club is not conducted during school hours, an adult should be within sight and hearing to provide some supervision, guidance and safety.

In the true sense of being an active member, of course you will be in the background, ready to give suggestions only when asked for them. But you will be at each meeting.

Your main function is to get each group started and to stay in in the back as the members grow able to conduct their activities independently. Your other function is to provide the legal amount of supervision for chemical and electrical experiments, and any other activity that could be dangerous or very messy.

So, you'll have to be there, but you can probably get your plan book or paper grading done while students are having their meetings, if they are not during school hours. You will probably end up listening because it can be very interesting and amusing.

First Aid for Ailing Clubs

In the unlikely case that a club is running down, the first thing to do is find out the reason. It may be because of a small membership or a lack of interest.

In the case of a small membership, it may help to study your class list for new people who might not be talented in the subject, but who may have an interest in it. If this fails, ask other teachers if they have a few capable or very interested students who would like to join. This can add pep to a sick club that is too small.

If a club has members who are losing interest, this is the time when your inactive membership becomes active. Meet with the leaders and give them some ideas, but best of all, try to stimulate them to think up their own ideas. Use some of the suggestions in this book, and get more reference and idea books in the particular field. Help the club leaders to plan a trip, a visit from a resource person or a new project. Spark their next meeting by participating actively.

If this does not work, it can only mean that some of the members really are not interested enough in the subject to enjoy the activities. Gently guide them into other groups where they can be more enthusiastic and interested. It is better to have less members and to weed out the bored ones.

But, let's not be negative. We're sure that your clubs will flourish, and the club members will be having such a good time they won't even realize how much they're learning.

Above all, include everyone in some special interest club. If you use your ingenuity, every child in your group can really be interested in some way.

Interclub Cooperation

Personal cooperation and an extension and enrichment of interests can occur if you encourage interclub cooperation. Many of your students will be able to help each other's projects by sharing time and talents.

If you have a club that concentrates on leadership and politics, the students in the language club can use their verbal talent to help them with campaign speeches and posters. The language people can use the talents of the class leaders to help them get the work done on time on a class newspaper.

The mechanically able group may build or invent some gadgets for sale, and they can ask the children in the art club to make posters to advertise their products. A group interested in business or sales may be recruited to help them as salesmen and to figure their profits.

A cooking or sewing club will need the help of other groups to advertise and sell its wares. These are just a few examples of the possibilities of interclub cooperation.

If an interesting speaker comes to visit, it is possible that two or more clubs might find the visit of interest. They would then get together to hear the speaker.

Your students themselves may think of other interclub projects. They may take field trips together and share a bus and its expense. For example, if the mathematics club, the mechanics club and the science club go to a museum such as the Museum of Science and Industry,* they might split up into club groups and go

---

*Museum of Science and Industry, E. 57th Street and Lake Shore Dr.; Chicago, Ill.

to separate exhibits there if their time is limited. If there is enough time, all the groups might visit the exhibits together, viewing things of interest to all of the clubs.

HOW TO AVOID HAVING AN ELITE GROUP

One big danger in working with a small group or club that has a special talent is in making its members so vain that you ruin their personalities. It is also very distressing to many of the other students to see one small group set aside for what seems to be special privileges.

There must never be an elite group. Since most children are talented in some special way, if we find and encourage this talent and interest we will have many groups, or clubs, of talented children, all of whom excel in a different way. Instead of *one* elite group, we will have many special groups, some in a state of flux as interests and talents grow and change. Every child in your class can participate as a member of a special group, if you encourage him to join. There are so many different ways that a child can be bright. Let each one shine in his own way.

CHECKLIST

* Allow pupils to select some of their own activities if they wish to, as this will give the work more importance.
* Add zest to your teaching with interclass special interest groups.
* Plan optional groupings in a self-contained classroom by scheduling one group at a time, or by alternating your time between two groups.
* Give generous encouragement to all creative efforts, as well as ample practice time.
* Plan creative writing and art projects, which go well together, for simultaneous projects.
* Find research and construction projects of two different models, as they can be a practical project for one teacher with two groups.
* Bring each child into some special interest club.
* Encourage children to join clubs that are closest to their interests, and to use clubs to develop new interests.

* Use tests, observation and listening to guide each student into the special club that best meets his needs.
* Use clubs to individualize by identifying pupils' interests and by giving you opportunities to work informally with them.
* Plan one special club meeting each day during an independent study time.
* Supervise every club meeting and stay in the background unless needed; but always be available for safety reasons, whether or not the club meets during school hours.
* Vitalize ailing clubs by planning trips and visits from resource people and by adding capable pupils from other classes.
* Stimulate clubs whose members are losing interest to generate their own ideas, and help with some of your suggestions.
* Guide bored members into clubs where they can be more enthusiastic and interested.
* Encourage clubs to meet and work together on special projects, and to use their talents to help each other.
* Avoid an elite group by having many different groups, so that each child can feel important.
* Use your ingenuity to help each child in your class to find interests and be talented in his *own* way.

7

Teaching with Individual Conferences

There are times when an individual conference is the best way, or the only way, to accomplish your educational purposes or to help a confused or troubled child.

Try to allow at least a half hour each school day, if you can, just for this purpose. There are so many worthwhile things that the rest of the class can be doing while you conduct these conferences. Spelling practice, handwriting practice, silent reading, research work, map drawing or art projects are only a few examples. A student helper can give a large group spelling test, or pairs of students can work as partners to test each other on individualized spelling lists. A child can read aloud from a story as a wonderful end to each afternoon, and you can conduct whispered conferences at this time. The children you are working with can always borrow the book the next day to catch up on the part of the story they missed.

The many kinds of conferences you may wish to conduct are as varied as all the subjects you teach and all of the individuals you will be talking to. The conference may be a planning session for a research project, a regular checking conference for individualized reading, an opportunity for you and a child to get to know each other, a final discussion and proofreading on a creative story, an evaluation meeting, an explanation and reworking of a mathematical problem, a planning period for a science experiment, a cooperative effort to solve a child's social problems, a motivating session to inspire a better attitude toward schoolwork, a chance for a student to tell you his troubles and get to feel better, a planning time for a newspaper staff member or a club leader, a personal request for a certain type of assignment; and of course, there are many other kinds of conferences.

This chapter will give suggestions on how to meet with everyone according to need. It will discuss follow-through conferences, give examples of good and poor conferences, suggest ways to improve individualized reading conferences and tell you what to do when you can't get to everyone who needs you.

HOW TO MEET WITH EVERYONE
ACCORDING TO NEED

You will never be able to meet with everyone who needs you at the very moment when he decides he needs help. So, it will be necessary to make decisions as to which child to meet with first and how long to meet with him.

In most cases, the only fair way is to decide to meet with the one who asks for help first. There will be times when many ask at once, or when you must make exceptions to this.

In such cases, use your knowledge of your students' personalities and learning abilities to select those whom you help first. If there are four or five students who seem troubled about a problem or snag in their work and each one needs a different kind of help, choose first the student who has a nervous type of personality. He is the least likely to work it out by himself without help or reassurance. The calm ones will either figure it out themselves or else not care if they don't. Then, for the next one to call up, select the slowest student as the one with the greatest need. If there are a few slow ones who need help and you do not think you'll get to all of them, choose the ones who must leave promptly to catch a bus, and keep the others for a few extra minutes.

If one child is waiting for help on a regular assignment and another wants a conference to discuss an individualized reading follow-up activity, choose the former as having the most pressing need. If two students are waiting to see you and you don't know what the conferences will be about, select the student by deciding which one has had the least amount of conferences recently. When two students need help and you must choose one, try to see first the one who can be helped only by you. Then, find another student to give help to the one who is waiting, using your knowledge of the helping child's capabilities.

There will be times when you may want to change your plans entirely. If you have just introduced a new concept and you have many requests for individual conferences at the same time for help with the concept, discontinue the individual conferences and call up a small group meeting for reteaching the concept.

FOLLOW-THROUGH CONFERENCES

It is very important for students' motivation in all work to know that their teacher cares how they are progressing. In the case of independent work, it is usually a necessity in order for the child to want to keep working at all. It is only the rare pupil who can keep going on his own for an extended period of time without a sign of interest from his teacher.

For this reason, it is essential to schedule regular conferences with all students who are working independently, even if the conference is just for a minute or two. It shows the student that you're interested, aware of his progress, available to give him help when he needs it and that the whole project is worth doing.

There are too many classroom situations in which the so-called "independent workers" are consistently copying from each other's workbooks, visiting instead of working, practicing skills incorrectly and causing discipline problems for their fellow students and teacher because of their boredom.

Individual conferences are your chances to correct errors, reteach and inspire. Independence and working at their own speed are necessary and worthwhile for the students, but only if their papers, projects, experiments and workbooks are checked at regular intervals. When the checked work is returned, this is an excellent opportunity for you to say a few words of encouragement or praise on the work's progress. If incorrect procedures are being practiced, this is the time to teach the correct ones, with a smile and a few words to motivate the student not to give up in discouragement.

If you can skim the pupils' work regularly, especially the independent work, you will prevent the sad situation of errors that

are practiced, identical errors in many workbooks because of copying, and wasted days because of a child's attitude of hopelessness
that the work is just being given to keep him busy.

Vary the types of conferences and the amount of time you devote to them, according to the learning situation. Individual conferences may be very brief, but they can inspire students to do
more work, to do better work and to do their *own* work.

EXAMPLES OF GOOD AND POOR CONFERENCES

Good

Ronnie came up when it was his turn.

"I can't spell *answer*."

"All right. I'll help you. Please bring up your dictionary."

"Here."

"O.K. What letter does *answer* start with?"

"*a.*" He turned to the *a* section.

"What comes next after *a*?"

"*n.*"

"Look for *an*." He found the combination by using guide
words, as he had been taught to do previously.

"I don't see the word."

"Look at the guide words again. They tell you what's on each
page."

"Oh." He pointed to the correct page.

"Fine. Now, the word is in alphabetical order on this page.
Look through all the words on this page, and maybe you'll recog-
nize it."

He studied each word, and then pointed to *answer* with a
worried look on his face.

"You found it. Great! Isn't it good to find it by yourself?"

The boy's face lighted up, and he copied the word correctly.

Good

"I can't spell *answer*."

"I'm having a conference now, but I'll help you in a few minutes. Get the dictionary ready in the meantime, and look for the
word while you wait."

"O. K."

(A few minutes later) "Oh, Mrs. Ashley, I found it by myself."

"Good."

Good

"I can't spell *answer*."

"I'm busy now, so I'll have to just tell you. *answer* (spelled out slowly for the child as he writes it down)

"Thanks."

"You're welcome. Come back up to my desk in fifteen minutes, with a dictionary. I'd like to show you again how to use it."

"O. K."

Good

"I can't spell *answer.*"

"I wish I could help you look it up, Ron, but I'm busy now. Would you like to wait for me, or would you like me to ask someone to help you?"

"I need it now."

"All right. I'd rather not just spell it for you. Mary, will you please help Ron look up his word? Use the guide words, and show him how to find the word by himself."

"Thanks."

Could Be Better

"I can't spell *answer*."

"*answer*" (spelled out for the child)

"Thanks."

Poor

"I can't spell *answer*."

"Go look it up."

Very Poor

"I can't spell *answer.*"

"Can't you see that I'm busy? When are you ever going to learn to use a dictionary?"

INDIVIDUALIZED READING CONFERENCES

Pupils who are engaged in individualized reading will have special conferences to check their oral reading, give vocabulary and phonics help, discuss follow-up activities for each book and their general reading progress.

Duplicate index cards are to be filled out for each book read. After doing this, the pupil gives one card to the teacher to be alphabetically filed by pupil's name in a small box. The other card remains in the child's book as a bookmark. It is handy for writing down as many new words as the pupil finds.

A typical card looks like the following:

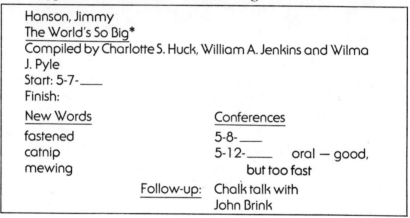

Figure 7-1

Encourage pupils to sign up on a conference sheet for reading help, follow-up planning or just to talk over the book. Ask children to look up new words on their own using a dictionary, and to ask you for help if they need it.

As often as possible (at least once a week), scan the alphabetical file in your box to pull cards on people you haven't seen lately. A notation of each conference date will keep you informed of this. Take out those cards which show no recent conferences, and use the cards themselves as reminders and for notations.

Expect each pupil to turn in a follow-up activity and a card with a finish date when a book is completed. In most cases, schedule the book's follow-up activity (oral report, review card, chalk

---

*Huck, Jenkins and Pyle (compiled by), *The World's So Big.*

talk, diorama, drawing, dramatized scene, decorated book jacket with review etc.), before the book is completely finished. In this way, the pupil can go right on to a new book.

Keep special question index cards on as many books as you can. Jot down a few questions about important ideas, situations or characters, noting page numbers when relevant. When a pupil chooses a book that you have a card for, keep the book question card with his name card so that you have it ready for his conferences.

When a child comes up for his reading conference, write down the date and check to see if you have a question card clipped to his name card. Try not to ask a question that applies to a section of the book that he hasn't read yet. Draw a small pencil line under the last question you ask, and file the question card behind his name card, ready for the next conference.

In case you have no question card and have never read the book, a good conference will result if you ask the child to read aloud a bit from the pages he has already read. You may wish to enter oral reading grades or comments on the card for future reference; for example, for extra help or for conferences with parents.

If the card is empty of new words, as most will be, after you have discussed the good points of the pupil's oral reading and have made suggestions for improvement, then flip only the pages of the book that have been read, and find difficult words to ask him about. If he doesn't know their meaning and has skipped them, briefly discuss each word (what it means and its pronunciation), and enter each of them on the card for future review. If time permits, ask the child to tell you what type of book it is, and how he feels about some of the main characters.

You may want to spend time helping the pupil plan his follow-up activity or in providing materials for it. If a chalk talk is planned, write the name of the pupil's partner on the card after making sure that the partner has already read the same book. Remind both children not to tell the ending, and to take turns telling only a *little* bit about the story, while the other person draws a *quick* line drawing or simple sketch on the board with colored chalk. Whenever a follow-up requires more than one person, all parties concerned should participate in the same conference, or in part of it.

Use the notes on your index card to check not only new vocabulary words and oral reading, but also any possible reading difficulties. For instance, if a pupil needs special work on long or short vowels, his card, with those of others with similar problems, will help you to organize a small group for extra instruction or needed practice.

Use the child's questions to guide you in your conference. Listen carefully and be ready to give any help that is needed. If time runs out, schedule a second conference soon.

It is good to check that follow-ups are completed, as this gives training to pupils in responsibility. You may not be able to keep up with some of your fast readers and have as many conferences or ask as many questions on each book as you would like. However, it is more important to allow the children to go on to other books and to maintain their enthusiasm in reading. Your index cards will help you to catch up on the pupils who are moving fast, and you'll be able to have great discussions on their next books.

WHAT TO DO WHEN YOU CAN'T GET
TO EVERYONE WHO NEEDS YOU

Since you can't get to everyone who needs you at the right time, it puts a great deal of pressure upon you, which you must try to lessen by the awareness that you're doing all you can. When you're calm and unruffled everything goes faster anyway.

Chapter Two also discusses how children sign up for individual conferences on sign-up sheets. Unfortunately, the X written before a name, or a hand waving in the air, is not always a signal of the greatest need. Some children will show great excitement and persistence, and even come up to interrupt an individual conference to ask a question. However, this may not indicate an urgent need at all, but just a persistent or excitable personality. The quiet child, the tense one, the bored child, or the one who doesn't care whether he's helped or not — these are the ones who probably have the greatest need. So, once you get to know who your most vocal and aggressive pupils are, refuse to allow them to monopolize your time, as they are sure to do if they can. Their urgency may be completely imaginary or trivial. Also, their great interest will assure them of help or an answer soon, anyway. These are the children whom you can refer to dictionaries, encyclopedias or other pupils for temporary help until you can meet with them.

Be alert for the daydreamer who gets almost nothing done. He's hoping that you won't notice him, or else he isn't even aware of you or what he should be doing.

Another child who needs help right away is the tense one who gets easily discouraged. He may run into one snag in his work and give up completely. If you can get to him soon you can build up his confidence and prevent a wasted school day. You will soon be able to differentiate between this type and the pushy child.

The pupil who is diligently working in the wrong direction needs you too. He is usually busy and quiet, but learning and accomplishing nothing. He may be doing great quantities of work incorrectly, practicing incorrect methods or memorizing incorrect facts. The only way to get to this kind of child is to check his workbooks, correct his papers and give frequent oral and written quizzes.

If the school day is almost over, and there are two or three children who really seem to need help urgently — it may be necessary to change your schedule and give the rest of the class a free reading period. Use this time to help the few who need it the most.

In case you give homework assignments, try to help first those who don't understand how to do the homework. There is nothing more upsetting for students or parents than an incompletely understood assignment. If you find it impossible to get to such a student before he or she must leave, then change the individual assignment to a practice one until you can explain the original homework.

Try to use part of an occasional recess period for individual conferences if they seem urgent and individual conference time is scarce. Five minutes from a recess is not that important, if you can help to reassure a child or explain something he's confused about.

Keep one or two children after school for a few minutes if you can't help them during the school day and they seem upset. In case they must make a bus, give them your school or home telephone number so they can talk to you when they get home. It may work out well to give a few special passes so troubled pupils can come in early the next morning before the rest of the class enters the building. A few minutes alone with you can change the whole outlook of a confused child.

If you consistently do all or some of these things, then try to forget the pupils who needed you that day and didn't get a chance to be helped. After all, tomorrow is another day.

Whatever else you hope to accomplish, you will also find conferences to be effective, enjoyable opportunities to know your pupils.

So, there are many different ways and reasons to have conferences. They can be very short and still do the job of telling you how a pupil is progressing, and telling the pupil that you care.

CHECKLIST

* Use individual conferences when they are the best, or only, way to help a confused or troubled child.
* Meet with individuals for various reasons, as conferences can serve an unlimited number of purposes.
* Try to help children in turn, but make exceptions for those who are upset or who are stopped in their work.
* Decide which child needs you the most, based upon individual temperament and capability.
* Discontinue individual conferences and teach a small group when you have many requests for the same help.
* Motivate independent workers by short individual conferences.
* Check on children's progress by skimming papers and workbooks, and by meeting regularly with pupils, especially those who are working at their own speed.
* Show pupils how to help themselves by teaching dictionary and other skills.
* Use pupil helpers when you can't have conferences with everyone who needs you, especially for spelling and dictionary help.
* Check with regular conferences in individualized reading, but don't worry if you're unable to discuss each book completely with each child.
* Use small group conferences for teaching needed reading skills and for helping partners with follow-ups.

* Refuse to allow aggressive students to monopolize your conference time.
* Watch for the daydreamers, the tense pupils, those who do little, children who never want help and those who work incorrectly.
* Meet with individuals whenever possible, even after school hours, if they need help.
* Relax about those students you didn't get a chance to help, because you will get to them tomorrow.

8

Case Study of Small Group Individual Enrichment — Group 1

Plan an enrichment project with a small group. You could meet with each unit of five pupils for about six weeks, until every child in the class has had a turn. While you're busy with the small group, the rest of the children could be doing vocabulary dictionary work to supplement their reading assignments.

DECIDING BETWEEN LARGE OR SMALL GROUP INDIVIDUALIZED ENRICHMENT PROJECTS

Small group work is very satisfying to the students and to you, but its demands on the teacher are much greater than those for large group study. Successful small group work requires individual attention to each group member, and extra checking if each person is working on a different topic. The rest of the class must be working independently while you accomplish this.

There will be times when a large group enrichment project will satisfy all of your goals. You can save time in initiating and motivating the work, and you can teach with individual conferences as the whole class works on its project. Each class member could choose his own topic, or the class as a whole could work on a topic or project.

In most cases of large group ventures such as the creative writing project described in Chapter Two, you will find that you will want to be flexible and mix large and small group procedures as they prove useful.

A good compromise between large and small group work can be to begin the motivating session with a large group lesson, break up the class into small groups working on similar subjects and culminate the project with large group sharing. An example of this procedure is given in the section "Planning Committee Research" in Chapter One. If you use this approach you can get the best from both methods.

The following anecdotal record will tell my adventures with the first of two different groups of five children.

INFORMING PARENTS ABOUT THE
ENRICHMENT PROJECT

Each of the parents had been notified about the special project with the following letter:

Dear Mr. and Mrs. _____:

     _____ is about to participate in a special "Enrichment Project." _____ will work on it with Mrs. Ashley and four other children twice a week for approximately six weeks.

     The project will begin with each child's choice of a subject or a question to study in depth. You can make an important contribution by discussing this choice with _____ and encouraging him (or her) to choose any field or question at all that really interests him (or her).

     The goals of this project are:

1. *motivation and increased pleasure in learning.*
2. *increased facility in research techniques.*
3. *increased desire and ability to work independently to learn more in depth about a topic.*
4. *interest in learning about related topics.*

     The children will select their own methods and media for sharing what they have learned with their class.

> *We hope that this will be an exciting, challenging experience for your youngster.*
>
>
>
> *Sincerely,*
>
> *Mary Osborne**
>

Figure 8-1

Monday, September 13, 19--

The children were eager to begin, and all of them had their topics chosen before they arrived. They had been told that they could study any subject they liked, but the pupils didn't know yet about a report to their classmates.

We talked about the many ways that they could tell their classmates about what they would learn. We all agreed that there were various ways to make it interesting for them, and that group members would decide later how they would like to present their reports.

CURIOSITY QUESTIONNAIRE

The children filled out a questionnaire as a help to themselves in deciding on their topics. We talked about the fact that they could take these sheets home, discuss their possible topics with their parents and make final decisions on Thursday. They wanted to tell me their topics, so I wrote them down on my list (in pencil), saying that they could still be changed Thursday. The topics were not filled in on their questionnaire.

NAME _____

AGE _____

What new things would you like to learn about?

_____

_____

_____

---

*Mary Osborne, Principal, Middlefork School, Sunset Ridge School District No. 29, Northfield, Ill.

What would you like to learn how to make?

_____

_____

What are some things that make you curious?

_____

_____

_____

Would you like to find out how some special thing is made? If so, name it. _____

What new kind of books would you like to read?

_____

_____

MY TOPIC _____

Figure 8-2

CHOOSING A TOPIC

Wednesday, September 15, 19--

I couldn't resist gathering a few materials ahead of time, even though the topics weren't set. I found four biographies of different presidents for Laura. She had tentatively chosen "The Lives of Presidents" for her topic, but had not narrowed it down to a few presidents. Jim had chosen "Indians of Illinois," and I had reserved a book in our own school library that might help him to get started. This book was not general, like most of the books about Indians, but told the names of specific tribes who lived in Illinois. The main reason why I started gathering extra materials was that I was so excited about the project that it was better to do something unnecessary rather than just wait.

Thursday, September 16, 19--

The topics were almost set!
Laura — "The Lives of Presidents." (not yet chosen)
Jim — "Indians of Illinois." (so far so good)
Susan — "Rocks." She had changed to this from "How the

Earth Was Made" after looking through some of the material. (We were both glad.)

Don — "Bees." He had switched to this after starting with 'Ticks."

Jerry — "Ancient Egypt." He had started out with "The History of Northfield," but he was worried that we wouldn't find much on the subject. (So was I.)

Well, we certainly have variety.

PLANNING RESEARCH

I told Laura about the books that would help her decide which presidents she wanted to study, and that she could make up her mind whether she wanted the books after she surveyed our school library's biographies.

Jim glanced through the book on Illinois Indians that would give him a start. We discussed the fact that he would find materials on Indians listed under Desert Indians, Plains Indians and Forest Indians. He told me he was sure we didn't have a desert in Illinois, but he knew that we had many forests in the early days. Now he could find materials by tribe or by the type of environment that the Indians lived in.

The children knew how to use a card catalog, and they decided to study all the materials they had at school first, and then look elsewhere for more. They were to begin by searching encyclopedias, trade books and filmstrips before they looked for other things.

This seemed like a good time to give a "quickie" lesson on note-taking. (A note-taking lesson would work out well as a large group lesson for the entire class.) I showed how to use index cards, and told them that it isn't fair to write down an idea copied from a book without the author's name and the title of the book — to give him credit. The children learned to try to write things in their own words, and not to use *everything* they found — just the most interesting things.

I gave each child in the group a large brown envelope with his name on it, to hold his notebook, cards, books etc. The children went in alphabetical order to the card catalog, with some looking through the filmstrip lists and others at the encyclopedias.

They promised to use the dictionary, or to ask for my help when they found words they didn't know.

HOW TO STIMULATE DEEP LEARNING

The group was working eagerly. Don found an article on bees in the *Britannica Junior Encyclopaedia.** He liked the drawings, but found the article difficult, so I suggested that he try *The World Book* too.† He had been intrigued by some transparencies for use with an overhead projector, so I loaned Don a marking pen, and made sure that the encyclopedia page was completely covered with plastic as he traced the pictures. (He refused to draw the bee's parts without tracing.) When we had to stop, I put away the half-finished transparency and took the marking pen with me, so no damage could be done to the encyclopedia in my absence. Don had a filmstrip on bees checked out to look at later through the filmstrip previewer in the classroom. Susan had a slow start because she switched topics, but she was very relieved to have an easier topic. Laura went home loaded with biographies to read, because she wanted to choose two or three presidents to study.

We had made a fine beginning, but we all hated to stop. Our group kept the folders in a special hidden place in the library, in case someone had extra time to study his topic.

Later, I phoned the community volunteer group‡ and signed up my five pupils for their respective topics. There was a possibility of getting a resource person to come to visit us, and I told them that we would probably want him to speak to a few classes.

I called the River Trail Nature Center** at one of the Forest Preserves nearby, as one of my previous groups had gone on a nature walk and had seen a fine exhibit in their small museum. The high point of our trip had been seeing a real beehive. I was told that the beehives were still there, and that I could bring my class any time.

° *Britannica Junior Encyclopaedia,* (Chicago: Encyclopaedia Britannica, Inc., 1964).

† *The World Book Encyclopedia* (Chicago: Field Enterprises Educational Corp., 1974).

‡ Volunteer Talent Pool, 620 Lincoln Ave., Winnetka, Ill. 60093.

**River Trail Nature Center, Forest Preserve District, 3120 Milwaukee Ave., Northbrook, Ill.

Then I called the Chicago Historical Society to arrange a tour to see exhibits about presidents;* and they have many exhibits about Lincoln and Washington.

Next, I called the Field Museum of Natural History.† They have exhibits on Indians, ancient Egypt and rocks, so we must plan on this visit. By then, I was tired of telephoning, but I was very pleased about the way the project had begun.

Monday, September 20, 19--

When I spoke to the head of the River Trail Nature Center early this morning, he promised a special talk just for us on bees and Indian artifacts.

Laura told me that she chose only John F. Kennedy for her topic, so that ruled out a trip to the Chicago Historical Society, as they had very little on John F. Kennedy.

Our very helpful school librarian‡ gave me information on instructional television, which is telecast from the local high school.** I found an interesting program that I might schedule for Laura to see. It contains Kennedy's Bay of Pigs statement to to the nation. They also have available a series of three programs on local history called "History of Wilmette." Jim will learn about Illinois Indians from the first telecast, so I'll surely schedule that one. They also have a telecast called "A Look at Lincoln," and although it isn't Laura's topic, she may want to see it anyway. I'll ask her about it.

Our trip to the River Trail Nature Center is set for next Monday. The children are all eager to go, and we will probably see exhibits for two research topics.

Don spent his morning session working on the transparency drawings for the overhead projector. He labeled the parts of the bee, enjoying this immensely. He was also glad to get a book on insects that I found at home.

I had found a book for Susan too — on rocks and minerals —

---

* Chicago Historical Society, North Ave. and Clark St., Chicago, Ill. 60614.

† Field Museum of Natural History, Roosevelt Rd. and Lake Shore Dr., Chicago, Ill.

‡ Helen Mitchell, Middlefork School, Sunset Ridge School District No. 29, Northfield, Ill.

**New Trier Television, New Trier East High School, Winnetka, Ill.

and she'll use it for reference. We looked at some fossil rocks under a magnifying glass. (I have a small collection at home.) She made out a list of the different kinds of rocks that we decided she needed for testing —light, dark, red, brown, shiny, dull and glassy. Susan has a collection at home too, so she'll bring that and look for others. She is also going to bring vinegar and an eyedropper.

When I showed her a piece of jade that I had found on a California beach, she assured me that she would love to polish it — that she loves hard work! So, she put on a smock and began. Long ago I had bought the equipment to polish the rock, and it included a typed list of instructions on how to do it. Now I was glad that I hadn't found the time for it. The equipment and instructions came from the Lizzadro Museum of Lapidary Arts,* a real treasure-house for rock lovers. With my help, Susan used the directions and the different types of sandpaper (identified by number), and wiped off the jade with a damp cloth after each sanding. The rock looked much more green when she was done, and she will finish the polishing later with a special rubbing compound. Susan is happy to know that the rock will become part of a lovely necklace.

Jerry was busy reading about Egypt. He got interested in hieroglyphics, and decided to copy some on a transparency for his report. The *World Book Encyclopedia* had some, but they were very small, so he used the magnifying glass to copy them. He plans to try another encyclopedia. I told him that we're sure to find hieroglyphics at the Field Museum of Natural History when we go.

Laura was intent on writing a report on John F. Kennedy. She told me that she plans to show pictures from the book, and perhaps trace some on a transparency for her report.

I called another school to borrow a rock collection for Susan. That school†is for the upper grades, while this one is only K-3.

Thursday, September 23, 19--

Everyone was present today. Jim commented that he had two good things this morning —our project and recess.

I had carried a heavy load of books in that I found at a local

---

*Lizzadro Museum of Lapidary Arts, 220 Cottage Hill, Elmhurst, Ill.

†Sunset Ridge School, Sunset Ridge School District No. 29, Northfield, Ill.

library —two for each child's topic. These were available for them to read at home, with one exception —a difficult book on ancient Egypt. I believed that Jerry should read this with a teacher nearby to help with the vocabulary.

Susan finished polishing the piece of jade, and it really looks different now. It's shiny and has a vein of white through the dark green. We've been showing the rock to anyone who will look. I brought in a pair of my own jade earrings to show to Susan, and we were both interested to note the differences in color and marking between the two varieties of jade. Susan brought in vinegar, an eyedropper and a pail full of rocks. We can hardly wait until we begin our testing.

The librarian found the rock collection that I had been inquiring about.* We were delighted, as each rock has a numbered label, keyed to a pack of numbered cards describing the rocks.

The other children in the group are becoming quite interested in the rocks too, and some want to help Susan collect more. We stored the rocks and equipment in one corner of the Materials Center until we can use them for testing.

Laura decided that she wanted to make a transparency picture for the overhead projector, and then Jim did too. Laura traced a picture of John F. Kennedy, and it came out well. Jim is drawing some different kinds of Indian picture writing.

All of the children were very happy to get their new books. Don is reading about bees and Laura is reading everything she can find about John F. Kennedy.

I asked Laura if she would like to see a TV program that had a small section showing President Kennedy talking to the nation about the Bay of Pigs. She thought it might be too old for her, so I didn't schedule it. We agreed that she may want to read about what happened at the Bay of Pigs.

Don asked me to try to get him some more filmstrips on bees. I suggested that he make sure he had seen all of our own filmstrips first.

I arranged for a videotape called "History of Wilmette" to be shown in our Materials Center, and I notified the librarian, who will turn the program on for the children. I invited Jim, who is

---

*"Rocks and Minerals of Illinois," Illinois State Geological Survey; Urbana, Ill.

interested in the Indians of the area, and Jerry, who wants to know all about the history of Northfield. Northfield is a suburb adjacent to Wilmette, and its early history will be similar to that of Wilmette, so Jerry should enjoy the program, even though Northfield is no longer his topic. This program is the first of the series, so Jim will surely learn something about the Indians who lived in this area.

A local museum, the Evanston Historical Society,* has artifacts of the Indians of Illinois, and many items about local history. I arranged a short visit for October 4.

Later that day, I mentioned to an acquaintance that I had a pupil who was interested in Illinois Indians. She told me that she had a map of the Indian villages and mounds in Illinois, and I arranged to borrow it. One of my friends heard our conversation, and she offered a book and a circular about the Dickson Mounds.†

Friday, September 24, 19--

When I got the map I noticed that it also shows chipping stations. I think that Jim will enjoy seeing it.

Sunday, September 26, 19--

My friend sent me a book about different Indian tribes, and a circular about the Dickson Mounds that shows photographs of excavations of prehistoric Indian houses and cemetaries.

Monday, September 27, 19--

Our group left for the River Trail Nature Center in high spirits. We had a beautiful warm day, and the children toured the Nature Center until the guide arrived. He led us to outdoor bee-hives and exhibits and gave us an interesting talk on bees. All of the children listened carefully, but took no notes. They had an opportunity to ask as many questions as they wished, and I was interested to see that everyone asked many questions.

Then the guide took us to a special outdoor exhibit on Indians who lived in this area. There was a wigwam made of bark, a

---

* Evanston Historical Society, 225 Greenwood St., Evanston, Ill.

† Dickson Mounds, The Dickson Mounds Museum, between Lewistown and Havana, Ill.; supervised by the Illinois State Museum, Springfield, Ill.

wooden drying rack for meat, a burial mound and pictures of a long house. Jim took careful notes on all of this.

When the guide left us, we took advantage of our opportunity to take a nature walk in the woods. We saw a pet rabbit, a raccoon, some chipmunks and many mosquitoes and yellowjackets.

We ate our sandwiches, but couldn't sit still too long, because yellowjackets were swarming all over the place. They may have been attracted to my cologne and Laura's sweet fruit juice. The children enjoyed the entire field trip very much.

Susan was eager about her rock testing and asked about it, so I told her that we would start it on Thursday.

Tuesday, September 28, 19--

I phoned another school, and a very helpful lady in charge of audio-visual materials said that she would send us some on our topics.* I urged her to find something besides books on John F. Kennedy. She thought that she had some cassettes with his voice, and I hope that Laura will be interested in them. The local educational television station told me they had no films on John F. Kennedy when I called to check.

IDEAS FOR ENRICHING EXPERIENCES

Thursday, September 30, 19--

The children arrived to see a table full of rocks, a wooden board, a hammer, vinegar, an eyedropper, a tile, rags and five pair of goggles. Laura had brought a book on rocks and minerals for Susan.

I asked the rest of the enrichment group whether they would like to join Susan and me in our rock testing, or work on their reports. There was no doubt about it, and they had to come too. (This type of activity can be done at recess or after school.)

We went to a far corner of the playground, set down the wooden board on the ground, and each child put on a pair of safety goggles. Susan chose a rock to break, completely wrapped it in the rags and hit it hard with the hammer, using the board. The first

---

*Martha Boos, Sunset Ridge School, Sunset Ridge School District No. 29, Northfield, Ill.

three rocks were too hard to break, but then Susan was able to break the rest. The other children had turns at hitting the rocks too, and we all examined the freshly broken surfaces of the rocks. Before we left, we separated the broken rocks from the unbroken ones and wrapped the broken ones in a rag.

Our caravan carried all the materials back into the building, and we set our rocks down on a long formica table. We borrowed a magnifying glass, because we were looking for the bubbles that would form if we poured vinegar on limestone. We didn't know how well the bubbles would show up on the white rock. Since we didn't know which rock (if any) was limestone, we had to try them all. Because we knew that limestone was nearly white, as we had seen it in our school collection, we could have eliminated testing everything but white rocks. However, the children were enjoying the testing so much that they wanted to test all of the rocks.

Susan spread the rocks on a piece of plastic and poured some vinegar into a paper cup. Laura held the magnifying glass while Susan poured vinegar from the eyedropper on each rock.

The vinegar just ran off all of the rocks until we came to one big white one that had fossil marks on it. Then, when Susan poured the vinegar on the raw, newly-broken surface of the rock, it fizzed and bubbled so much that we all got very excited! We didn't even need the magnifying glass. Now that Susan knew we had a piece of limestone, we could have stopped the vinegar testing, but we poured some more on because it was fun to watch it bubble. Then Susan made out a label for limestone and wrapped the limestone up in plastic with its label.

The next kind of test was to try for the color of streak a rock would make when rubbed hard against a white tile.* Some of the hard rocks made no mark at all on the tile, but when Susan finished she had a pile of rocks that made a black streak, one that made a white streak (we could see the white powder) and one that made a dark green streak. Labels were made out for the colors, and we wrapped the rocks in plastic.

The next time we test rocks it will be for hardness. The purpose of these tests is to show the various ways that rocks are de-

---

*Try to get an unglazed tile. If you can't, use the back of a glazed one.

scribed and separated into categories. We don't hope to be able to name them all.

Monday, October 4, 19--

The Volunteer Talent Pool has a speaker who could come to talk on "Prehistoric Indians," but I told them that I'd like to see if Jim was interested in this before we made arrangements. Later, I asked Jim about the speaker and he didn't seem to want to hear about "Prehistoric Indians." (I even checked to make sure he knew what prehistoric meant.) I notified the Volunteer Talent Pool.

The children were excited about the visit to the Evanston Historical Society. We arrived after a noisy trip, and a guide took us around, showing us the home of Charles G. Dawes, who was Vice-President of the United States under President Calvin Coolidge.

We saw mementos of Evanston's history and the Chicago fire; and costumes of the time. The children got interested in the Chicago fire. Jim asked, "Why are you celebrating its anniversary? It wasn't a good thing." The guide did quite well in explaining that you remember dates of important events, even if they weren't good. We saw antique dolls, an old music box and a collection of realia of the Potawatomi Indians of this area. Their beadwork was ornate and softly-colored; different from any we'd seen before. There were arrowheads, clothing and pottery. Jim was very busy taking notes.

It was a small place, so we didn't stay long. On the way back to school Don wanted to know if the queen bee and the drones made honey, and I said that only the workers made it. Then he asked me if honeybees were the only kind of bees that made honey, and I told him about bumblebees and how they didn't live in hives. I mentioned that they lived on clover, but that I wasn't sure about their honey. We all decided to look them up. Then Don asked whether hornets and yellowjackets made honey. My answer was that they didn't, as these insects weren't in the bee family — that they were wasps.

I told my group that they would have an opportunity to work on their reports on Thursday. I also asked Laura if she would like to see a telecast about Lincoln, and since she said that she would,

I'll arrange it. Later, I went to a library and collected some more books on the children's topics.

I looked up bumblebees in the encyclopedia, and found out that they are larger than honeybees, they live in smaller groups and they make honey which is too strong-tasting for people to want to eat. This is proving to be very educational (for me).

Thursday, October 7, 19--

I arrived loaded with cassettes, pamphlets, pictures, books, filmstrips and a record. The pupils were delighted, and they went to work with enthusiasm.

The librarian commented on how excited the children were about their projects. I agreed, saying they were even *fluttery.*

The youngsters took many of the materials home. Jim asked to have the Dickson Mounds pamphlet again, as his parents might take him there.

Susan was drawing a transparency of a geode, so I offered to bring one of mine to show her. When I showed Susan the completed jade necklace, one of the other teachers, who had heard about Susan's project, said that she wished that she could send some of her pupils to me for enrichment. She has one boy in particular who is interested in rocks, and she asked if he could come to one of our sessions. I invited him to the one a week from today, when we will test rocks for hardness. The teacher invited Susan to come and tell her class how she polished the jade. Susan seemed eager to go, so we arranged it.

I'm beginning to realize that with the great interest in their own topics, the field trips and the expanding interest in each other's subjects, we don't have enough time planned for the project. We'll have to extend it by a week.

On the way home I picked up some pamphlets on Indians and honeybees at the library. I also arranged for a telecast on Abraham Lincoln for Laura.

Friday, October 8, 19--

I went to a nearby library and I checked their picture files on each of our topics. I couldn't find "Rocks" and "John F. Kennedy," but the librarian helped me to find "John F. Kennedy" under "Biographies" and I found some good material under "Gems."

Tuesday, October 12, 19--*

We were off to the Field Museum of Natural History. When we arrived we toured the section on the archaeology of Egypt first, as Jerry has had no opportunities to see anything about his topic on our trips. The children were all impressed with the replica of the Rosetta Stone and how it was used as a dictionary to unlock the secrets of ancient Egypt. They were fascinated and horrified by the mummies.

After an early lunch we visited a room that has gems. Susan tried to take too many notes and to draw pictures of nearly everything she liked, so everyone else tired of the room and she was still at it. When the guard saw how interested she was he pointed out a very new gem, called *Tanzanite,* just discovered in Tanzania, Africa. It was a vivid blue, and he told us there were very few of them in the world. Then I began taking notes, and Jim wandered over and started taking notes about Tanzanite too. The guard discussed the various colors and uses of diamonds with us. Jim asked him some very penetrating questions about what it takes to cut a black diamond, since only a diamond is hard enough to cut a diamond. It's amazing how interested Jim is becoming in rocks.

When we finally left that room we looked at meteorites and minerals of all kinds, some fluorescent under ultra violet light. We walked on, saw a little theater, and took a rest as we viewed a film on Tibet.

Then we toured the exhibit on "Plains and Woodland Indians." The children were tired, so most of us rested while Jim took careful notes on the woodland Indians, and he didn't miss one display. At the souvenir counter Jim bought a color postcard showing a giant topaz he had admired in the Gem Room. Then we left for home.

The principal had good news when I arrived at the school. The Volunteer Talent Pool has a speaker for us on the subject of Indians, and she has posters and objects of interest to pass around. We may end up with three classes hearing her.

---

*We met on Mondays, but switched to Tuesdays when Mondays were holidays.

Thursday, October 14, 19--

Before we began testing rocks, we invited the boy from the other class, and I showed the children my two geodes that I had brought from home. One of them has an amethyst center.

We discussed the hardness scale of 1-10 that we were going to use to classify our rocks. The children all understand that 1 is the hardness number of the softest rock, and that 10 is the number of the hardest (diamond). They know that rocks can scratch, or make a mark on, all softer rocks having a lower number.

We began testing by scratching all the rocks with our fingernails. When we found some that scratched easily, we put them in a box marked 1. There were a few that scratched, but not easily, so they were put in the 2 box. Then we tried a penny on the remaining rocks. We couldn't find any that were scratched by the penny, rubbing it hard, so we didn't have a 3 box. The steel knife was used next, and the rocks it scratched easily were put in the 4 box.

The rocks that the steel blade would scratch when pressed hard were put in the 5 box. The rocks that could scratch the blade of the knife were put in 6. The last test was on a piece of glass, and the rocks that scratched the glass were placed in a box marked 7-10. We knew that they were at least as hard as 7, but they could be even harder. We joked about using my diamond ring for testing.

Another teacher came in to watch, and Jim answered some of her questions. He told her how black diamonds were used to cut other diamonds, (he learned that at the museum) and she was impressed. Jim commented that he has learned more about rocks than he has about Indians, but he seemed very happy about it.

I showed Susan how to test rocks by smell. She wet a piece of shale and noticed its strong smell of mud. Now she knows how to identify shale by its dark color and its smell. Susan is going to do this on her own, because we ran out of time. I left the jade necklace and polishing equipment with her, as she is going to tell another class about how she polished the stone. Today was fun.

Monday, October 18, 19--

Don had found (or killed) a yellowjacket and he asked me to get the Bio-View* machine that I had pointed out to him, so that

---

*Bio-View, H.H. Industries, Inc., Weston, Conn.

he could show the yellowjacket to the class during his report. I welcomed this expansion of interest, as it was related to his topic, and good learning.

I told my researchers that they would have only one more session to work on their reports before they were given, and I promised Don that we would work with the Bio-View machine on Thursday. I commented to the group that after the reports, we would fill out forms and talk about how we could make them even better.

Susan remarked, "I wish this group wouldn't be over next week." I told her that it didn't have to be — that she could continue to study about rocks and use the rock collection after her report, on her own.

I gave Don some printed information on bees that I had received when I went to a festival at Claysville, Illinois, and I gave Laura a map of the New Salem area showing the New Salem State Park, which had a restoration of the village where Lincoln had lived.

Thursday, October 21, 19--

There was a bustle of activity today since the children knew this was their last chance to work with me on their reports.

I had the Bio-View machine set up with a slide, ready for Don to try it out with the yellowjacket he had. The insect didn't show up well on the tiny screen of the machine, so I suggested that he put just one wing on the slide. It made a beautiful transparent picture on the screen. Don wanted to try it with a leg, but I told him to wait until next Tuesday, just before the report, so the leg wouldn't get lost.

Jim was looking at a filmstrip when our time was up, and he said, "I'm not going to recess. This is more fun." What a nice way to end the session.

SHARING WITH THE REST OF THE CLASS

Tuesday, October 26, 19--

A volunteer is due to talk to two classes about rocks. A speaker will also come to talk about bees, but he prefers to come in the spring and bring a hive.

Everything was all set for the reports on Thursday.

While waiting for the speaker to arrive, Susan and I showed the pictures of gems that she had chosen. The volunteer gave an interesting talk and passed around specimens of limestone and shale. (It might have been better if he had waited until his talk was over to do this, as it distracted the children from listening to him.) He spoke about glaciers and how they left sand, gravel, and clay. I learned that gold is usually found in quartzite.

The children wrote thank you notes to the speaker after he left, and I wrote a note to the Volunteer Talent Pool. (There isn't enough class time for the pupils to write all the thank you notes that are needed.)

Thursday, October 28, 19--

We were all set. The rock collections, geodes and rock testing equipment were on display, and the Bio-View machine was ready with a slide. The screen was down, the overhead projector in place and the first overhead visual was on it, ready to show.

I planned to have Jerry do his talk first, as he is a very tense child and I didn't want him to wait too long. At the start he acted very embarrassed and made a few joking remarks which caused the audience to laugh at some of the serious things he was saying later; but then they settled down. Jerry spoke using note cards occasionally. The cards had a list of things he wanted to tell. He told about King Tut* (we shortened the name for him because he couldn't pronounce it), and showed a book about Tut's treasures. After each important item he asked for questions. Jerry told about other Pharaohs and how they were regarded as gods as well as rulers, and he spoke of the pyramids. When his report was over, I suggested that he show Egypt on the map. He did this and went on to speak some more. I was impressed with his ability to talk most of the time without any notes at all, and he sounded enthused about his subject.

Susan began her talk with an overhead visual showing a pic-

---

*King Tutankhamon

ture of a geode. She displayed my two geodes and said that she didn't know where I got them. I remarked that I had bought them at the Lizzadro Museum of Lapidary Arts in Elmhurst, Illinois. Then Susan showed the jade necklace and the sandpaper, and told how she had polished the jade. She demonstrated the streak test on a piece of white tile, with the rocks that had made a black streak and a white streak. Susan showed the limestone test, then told about the test for hardness and answered questions about it, explaining what the numbers 1-10 meant. She did well, going into detail about the fingernail test that separates No. 1 rocks because they are so soft, and ended by enthusiastically mentioning the Field Museum trip. Susan used no notes at all, speaking naturally and showing her great interest. I mentioned that the entire class could see the exhibits up close when all of the reports were over.

Jim spoke about a few Illinois Indian tribes, and then gave some facts about their homes. He glanced at his notebook once in a while, but did not read aloud from it. He sounded very nervous and his talk was brief.

Don showed pictures and explained them well. He started to show the overhead visual with pictures and labels of parts of the bee, when a fuse blew, so I suggested that he show the transparency tomorrow and go on with the rest of his report. He showed a part of a wasp's nest, and then he put a wing and a leg of the yellow-jacket on the slide of the Bio-View machine. Luckily, the electricity was working again, and they appeared on the small screen of the machine. Don showed his overhead visual of the bee and everyone was very interested. He spoke without any notes at all.

I gave Jim his map of Illinois which located all the former Indian villages and chipping stations, and I asked him if he would like to show it. He wanted to, so he had a second opportunity to speak, explaining the map and telling the class that he was going to display it.

SUGGESTIONS FOR EVALUATION

Later, after I had praised all of the speakers, I asked my group to fill out evaluation forms on each other's reports. We discussed each report in a positive way after the forms were filled out.

PROJECT REPORT

NAME OF PUPIL WHO GAVE THE REPORT _____
WHAT I LIKED ABOUT THE REPORT _____
_____
_____
_____
_____

I THINK THE REPORT COULD HAVE BEEN EVEN BETTER BY _____
_____
_____
_____
_____

Figure 8-3

One comment on Jerry's report was:

WHAT I LIKED ABOUT THE REPORT *I liked the hole report becose he said it good.*

Jerry wrote this about his own report:

I THINK THE REPORT COULD HAVE BEEN EVEN BETTER BY *not make it funny.*

We all agreed that everyone spoke well, without reading their reports. I was glad that, earlier, I had given the group a silly, little horrible example of someone reading a report quickly in a monotone without looking up. They had laughed at me at the time, but it must have made an impression.

All the children agreed with me that Susan's report was great, and that she had an advantage by having the geodes, rock collections and testing equipment to show. They all thought she could have improved the report by not being so nervous. We decided that we were *all* nervous, and that the best way not to be nervous in the future was to have lots of practice in talking before a group. One child said it could have been better by "talking more about the things she talked about." Susan made this comment about her own report:

I THINK THE REPORT COULD HAVE BEEN EVEN BETTER BY *having more things to show. (pictures of gems that she had forgotten at home)*

One child said this about Jim's report:

WHAT I LIKED ABOUT THE REPORT *I liked it all. It was very short but it was very good! GREAT!*

Jim said this about his own report:

I THINK THE REPORT COULD HAVE BEEN BETTER BY *I could have had it longer.*

Some comments about Don's report:

WHAT I LIKED ABOUT THE REPORT *The thingy mubob, but it all was GREAT!*

(He meant the Bio-View machine.)

WHAT I LIKED ABOUT THE REPORT *I liked the hole report. Don had lots of interesting things to tell about, stuff that I didn't even know.*

I told the children again that they had all done a fine job. Then I collected as many books, pictures and pamphlets as I could, asking that everything be in next session.

I was pleased because the group had shown great interest in their own and in each other's topics. One mother wrote me, "I'm so glad to finally see a special project where the emphasis is *not* on the report."

An extra benefit from our project has also come up. Some of the other pupils who showed no interest in independent projects before have asked to do one. I call this "constructive jealousy."

It was time to leave. The children had made the reports, but *I* went home tired. We all felt great about the whole project.

Monday, November 1, 19--

The speaker from the Volunteer Talent Pool did such a fine job that she held the group's interest for almost an hour, when some of the classes had to leave for lunch. One teacher and class stayed on to ask even more questions.

The volunteer demonstrated and explained an Indian sand painting. She spoke about the Potawatomi Indian tribe and showed colored posters about Indian homes, cradles and art. She told how Indians collected wild rice and maple syrup. A collection of realia was described and passed around for everyone to see: a small Indian war club, beading, a basket and porcupine quill embroidery. She gave examples of the Potawatomi language, which is only oral, not written. She also told some charming stories that were used to teach lessons to children.

I learned many new things, and some of them are given here:
— The word "chief" is a European concept. It is a name given to the Indians who made most important decisions in a group. Old men or great hunters had the most prestige, and they would be consulted more than the others, so they were called "chiefs."

— Indian wives carried the loads so that the men would have their arms free for using their bows and arrows to shoot game or protect the group.

— Baskets are used instead of pottery by hunting people because they are lighter to carry and don't break. The farming Indians of the west made pottery.

— Birch bark was used for canoes because it made the canoe light to carry on the long portages.

— Indian children are not spanked or scolded; and they are taught how to behave by stories that teach lessons of cause and effect.

The speaker was deluged by questions, and Jim's was the first. He asked, "How did they light the fires? Did they really rub sticks together?" Answer: "Yes. They also used a stone called a *flint* so they could light the fire quickly." One child asked where the speaker got her information. Answer: "From a man who belongs to the Potawatomi tribe."

The children wrote thank you notes to the speaker, and I wrote one to the Volunteer Talent Pool.

That evening I phoned Jim's mother and told her about an Indian powwow I had heard advertised on FM radio. It was sponsored by the American Indian Center of Chicago,* so it would be authentic. I spoke to her after Jim's bedtime, because I didn't want to tell him about it unless he could go. She was very interested in taking him.

---

*American Indian Center Inc., 1417 W. Wilson Ave., 1630 W. Wilson Ave., Chicago, Ill.

Thursday, November 4, 19--

Since Laura was absent last week, she gave her report today. It was very brief. She started out by reading it and wisely cut it short. Last of all, she showed an overhead visual picture of John F. Kennedy and some library pictures of both Kennedy and Lincoln.

In our evaluations everyone said that they liked Laura's report. Her own comment was:

WHAT I LIKED ABOUT THE REPORT *the pichers*

Some other opinions of Laura's report:

I THINK THE REPORT COULD HAVE BEEN EVEN BETTER BY: *telling about what she knew without reading papers.*

I THINK THE REPORT COULD HAVE BEEN EVEN BETTER BY: *just a little more about the things she told about.*

The group agreed that all of the reports had been good.

I told the enrichment children that I was very proud of their work, and that today was our last special class. I began to get excited about the new group that would start next.

Looking back, I realized that I had done a great deal of work with my enrichment group, but I know that it was well worth it — for the children and for me.

CHECKLIST

* Compromise in large group enrichment projects by using small groups, large groups and combinations of the two as needed, to get the best of both methods.
* Inform parents about the enrichment project — its procedure and its goals.
* Help students choose their own topics by having them think about what makes them curious.
* Teach ethical and efficient note-taking procedures.
* Use volunteer talent and any community resources available.
* Give pupils opportunities to manipulate and experiment with objects related to their topics.
* Allow group members to share each other's topics when they are interested.

* Be flexible and allow more time if the project requires it.
* Place the greatest project emphasis on what is done and what is learned; not on the reports.
* Help children with their projects when you can, with suggestions and materials.
* Share in constructive evaluation of the reports.

9

Case Study of Small Group
Individual Enrichment — Group 2

My second enrichment group consisted of five other children. Everything was planned for them in the same way that was described in Chapter Eight.

The group was also scheduled to meet twice a week for about six weeks. This length of time was set in order to allow enough time for each child in the class to have a turn to participate.

While I met with the special group, the rest of the class worked on their regular reading and spelling assignments. The children in the enrichment group were required to make up this work, using some of their free periods.

PLANNING RESEARCH TOPICS

Tuesday, Nov. 9, 19--

We talked about the project, and the children filled out the Curosity Questionnaires (See Figure 8-2.), put them in their pockets to take home, and began to talk about possible topics. With the understanding that the topics can be changed until Thursday, they made tentative plans.

Grancy — race cars or machines

Mitch — fossils or dinosaurs

Roosevelt — automobiles, fossils, dinosaurs or insects

Pam — collage

Gail — dramatics or dinosaurs

I decided to try to make use of the remaining class time even though the topics were very tentative. The group went to the library, where the librarian gave them a short lesson on using the card catalog to find books and films. We were lucky that she had no class at that time and could help the children too. My pupils looked for books on all of their possible topics and read through them avidly. Before their time was up they were checking out piles of books. (I learned from the last group that children can decide on a topic easier once they have seen books on the various subjects they're considering.)

Pam couldn't find any books on collage, but the librarian helped her look it up in the encyclopedia. Later, I told Pam about my own book of one hundred collages that I made for an art course, and she is looking forward to seeing it. I also plan to bring one of my own books on insects, and a book about dinosaurs for whoever chooses the topic.

We were off to a good start, as the children were very excited about the project. Pam could hardly believe that she would be allowed to make collages for her project if she wishes to.

Thursday, November 11, 19--

The children were all set on their topics until Roosevelt changed from "Automobiles" to "Chemistry." This was after he had looked over some of the material on automobiles with Grancy. Grancy stuck to his "Automobiles," which will be a challenge for *me.* Pam chose "Collage," Gail wanted "Dinosaurs," and Mitch chose "Prehistoric Times." He plans to study both cavemen and animals of the time. It sounds as if we have interesting activities ahead of us.

HOW TO PREPARE AND MOTIVATE

Pam and Gail enjoyed looking through my book of collages, and we made plans for each of them to do a collage Tuesday. Grancy, Roosevelt and I read an article in an encyclopedia on "Automobiles" (I read it aloud) and we discussed Henry Ford, assembly lines and interchangeable parts. Mitch started out by reading a book about prehistoric life that I had brought for him. Then he got interested in the automobile discussion and joined us.

Friday, November 12, 19--

I phoned the Volunteer Bureau of Evanston* to request resource people on the five topics. Then I also sent an SOS to the Volunteer Talent Pool† on the "Automobile" topic.

In order to avoid bad weather, I decided to plan our trips as soon as possible. I made a reservation for the Museum of Science and Industry,‡ and they promised to send me their guide (mentioned in Chapter Three).

A man from the Volunteer Bureau called, and he will speak about "Prehistoric Life."

Tuesday, November 16, 19--

It took two trips from the car to carry all the books and chemistry and art supplies into the school. I stopped in to see our helpful librarian and coordinator,§ who had gathered some interesting materials on prehistoric life for us. We have a transparency book with twelve color transparencies and four duplicating lesson pages.** The lessons include a crossword puzzle, identification of pictures, two review quizzes and a Teacher's Guide. Mitch and Gail can do some of the lessons and read the transparencies. They might decide to show some of these materials for their reports to the class.

Another great group of materials are two sets of printed originals for preparing overhead projection transparencies. They are about "Prehistoric Man" and "Primitive Man."*** The children could read these printed originals. If they wish to show any for their reports, I will make up overhead visuals. "Prehistoric Man" compares the physical characteristics of early man with those of modern man. The traits that distinguish man from the

---

* Volunteer Bureau of Evanston, 828 Davis St., Evanston, Ill.

† Volunteer Talent Pool, 620 Lincoln Ave., Winnetka, Ill.

‡ Museum of Science and Industry, E. 57th St. and Lake Shore Dr., Chicago, Ill.

§ Donna Secrist, Librarian and Coordinator, Willard School, District No. 65, Evanston, Ill.

**Edward Ortleb and Richard Cadice, "Prehistoric Life," (St. Louis, Mo.): Milliken Publishing Co., 1968).

***Paul D. Swanson, "Prehistoric Man," Anthropology No. 1, Catalog No. 321; and "Primitive Man," Part 1, Anthropology No. 2, Catalog No. 322, 3M Co., Education Services, Box 3100, St. Paul, Minn. 55101.

animals are presented, as well as some of the early developments in his progress toward cultural sophistication. "Primitive Man," Part 1, illustrates many of the developments that have evolved in man's quest for food, shelter and clothing.

There are also two film loops* about dinosaurs which the children will be able to view on the projector.

I collected test tubes in a holder and more construction paper, and I prepared for a busy session.

We had a note-taking lesson, and discussed giving an author credit for his work, and not copying from a book. The children were told to write the information in their own words.

I gave out individual folders, note cards, books and pamphlets to each one in the group, telling them that all of their materials were recorded on my list. Then I gave the children a choice of working on collage or chemistry experiments for this session. The boys chose demonstrations† — the girls wanted to do collage.

The collage workers started immediately with the bagful of assorted cloth, wallpaper, yarn, cotton, buttons, construction paper etc. They each produced excellent unfinished collages which I kept for them, as they hope to work on them again.

Grancy, Mitch, Roosevelt and I used one of the chemistry books to do three experiments.‡ I helped them by reading the experiments aloud, as they had difficulty. Roosevelt wrote his initials with vinegar on white construction paper, and then he let them dry. We didn't have a pen and holder, so he used a toothpick. The first time he did it, he held the paper the required distance from the candle flame and the paper scorched. Roosevelt did it again, holding the paper farther from the flame. Our invisible ink worked, as we could then read his initials.

While the vinegar initials were drying, we used two test tubes in a stand to show the effect of soap on oil. Roosevelt poured one inch of water in a test tube. He added one inch of salad oil, covered the end of the test tube with his hand and shook it. The oil and

---

"Dinosaurs — Meat Eaters," 81-983, "Dinosaurs — Plant Eaters," 81-982, Ealing Film Loops, Walt Disney Nature Library, 1956; Walt Disney Productions, Glendale, Calif.

†We discussed the difference between demonstrations and real experiments in which the real results are unknown.

‡Mae and Ira Freeman, *Fun with Chemistry* (New York: Random House, 1944), pp. 18, 20, 54.

water separated and the oil floated on top. He mixed a half tea-spoon of soap powder in a half cup of water. Then he used this mixture to fill one inch of the second test tube with soapy water. He added one inch of salad oil, covered the tube's opening and shook the tube. This test tube looked creamy and the oil didn't separate from the water until later. It really showed how soap works to clean up oil.

Our other experiment demonstrated the way fire uses up oxygen. Roosevelt crumpled up a six-inch square of newspaper into the bottom of a small narrow glass. We prepared a soup dish with a small amount of water. I set the newspaper in the glass on fire and quickly turned the glass over, setting it up in the water inside the soup dish. We watched as the fire went out, the glass filled with smoke and the water in the dish disappeared. As the smoke cleared we saw the water had risen in the glass. We discussed how the oxygen in the glass had been used up by the flame, causing the air pressure outside the glass to be greater than the pressure inside. This pressure pressed down on the water, pushing it up into the glass. Roosevelt and the girls helped me clean up from the demonstrations and art work.

The boys enjoyed working with the chemistry materials. Grancy said, "I wish we could do this all day." Roosevelt offered to bring a glass that looked more like the glass in the book's illustration so that we could try the oxygen demonstration again.

In the afternoon I went to a wallpaper store and asked for an old book. The book I got will be great for collage.

I made out and mailed trip slips for next week's trip to the Museum of Science and Industry. Miss Secrist had spoken to the principal* for me about the problem of getting so many trip slips back in time. In case the child forgot to bring it back he would miss a trip, as most of the mothers are not home during the day. The principal said that I could put more than one trip on a slip. Miss Secrist and I decided it would also be wise to mail the trip slips home, asking that they be mailed back right away. This would involve an enclosed stamped self-addressed envelope, but it would be worth it.

---

*Dr. David A. Hagstrom, Principal, Willard School, District No. 65, Evanston, Ill.

WHAT TO DO WHEN THE PUPIL KNOWS MORE
ABOUT THE TOPIC THAN THE TEACHER

Wednesday, November 17, 19--

When I spoke to Mr. G _____, the volunteer speaker, he mentioned that he had taught woodworking and shop. I told him of my problem of not knowing enough about automobiles to do a good job of helping Grancy with his topic. Mr. G _____ suggested coming in to work with Grancy on a model car, and he offered to purchase one for me. I was delighted, and when he said he didn't mind if the other two boys watched, I planned on the girls working on collages at that time. I have the chemistry supplies ready too, but I think that Roosevelt and Mitch will want to share this experience with Grancy.*

I received the museum's guidebook, and I used it to plan Tuesday's trip.

Thursday, November 18, 19--

When I arrived loaded with chemistry supplies, wallpaper book etc., I met Mr. G _____ and introduced him to my group. He worked with Grancy and the other two boys chose to watch.

The two girls finished up their collages and started another. They made liberal use of some glitter, fabric and buttons, and the collages seemed very creative. The girls were delighted with the wallpaper book and old greeting cards that I brought.

Roosevelt and Grancy watched and helped Mr. G _____ work on the model car with rapt attention. As Mitch lost interest, I gave him the two film loops on dinosaurs. He went to the library for the projector while I taped a piece of white construction paper to the wall for a screen. (I had anticipated this, so I brought the loops and some tape.)

By this time, Mr. G _____ had decided that the model car he brought was much too difficult to start on, so he is going to buy a simpler car model tonight. He will come in tomorrow to work with Grancy and Roosevelt and let them both help.

---

*The girls were not interested in automobiles.

The entire group watched the film loops, which were colorful and exciting. After that, Roosevelt and Grancy looked through a large, heavy book on early automobiles* that I had borrowed. (I brought it just in case the volunteer couldn't come.) Mitch read a book on dinosaurs.

The children seemed excited about what they (*and the others*) were doing. Roosevelt told me about an experiment that he did at home. "It worked!" he said. He also remembered to bring a glass for the oxygen experiment. He is getting interested in dinosaurs and suggested switching topics, but I told him to stick to his own — that he would get to learn about dinosaurs too, with our speaker, and our trip to the museum† .

Miss Secrist told me about a fine film on dinosaurs, so I asked her to order it.‡ We'll show the film after the speaker leaves, as it will make a good follow-up.

She also gave me Dr. Hagstrom's answer to my question about a service station — he suggested a nearby one that did his work. He knew the owner well and felt that he would show the boys something about the workings of a car, no matter what was going on at the station.** I'll stop in tomorrow.

The district's Learning Resources Center had some materials (records, filmstrips, books) on machines and dinosaurs, which I borrowed. I marked them with the children's names and left them in the library for the youngsters to use in their spare time.

Friday, November 19, 19--

Mr. G _____ worked with Grancy and Roosevelt this morning, and they finished the car.

The confirmation came from the Field Museum, so we're set for that. They also sent floor plans and some "Treasure Hunt" question sheets, one of which is called "The Natural History of Prehistoric Reptiles." I'll bring it and try using it with the group.

I asked the girls whether they wanted to visit a service station

---

*Clarence P. Hornung, *Portrait Gallery of Early Automobiles* (New York: Harry N. Abrams, Inc., n.d.).

†Field Museum of Natural History, Roosevelt Rd. and Lake Shore Dr., Chicago, Ill.

‡ "Dinosaurs — the Terrible Lizards," 1970, 11 min., color. Charles Cahill and Associates, Hollywood, Calif.

**Bob Thorsen's Service Station, 2949 Central St., Evanston, Ill.

with us after school one day, but they weren't interested. Then I stopped in at the station and talked to the owner, who was very pleasant and cooperative. We set a date for a Monday, when he will show the boys the inside of an automobile and explain something about it. I made a note to ask the boys to wear old clothes that day, just in case they get to touch some of the parts and tools.

I brought home a duplicate of one of the books on automobiles that Grancy is reading, as I decided that I must learn *something* about the mechanics of a car. I chose the simplest book I could find.*

Saturday, November 20, 19--

While out with some friends, I spoke of my enrichment group and their topics, and I mentioned that I wished I knew more about model cars so that I could help Grancy more. Our friends got very excited about the idea of having their eleven-year-old son, Bradley, come to work with Grancy. They suggested this because model cars are his hobby. They assured me that he would enjoy doing it, and that it would be valuable enough for him to warrant excusing him from school for a few hours.

Sunday, November 21, 19--

Bradley called me about coming to help Grancy, and we set a date.† He offered to buy an inexpensive model for the boys to put together. (Roosevelt would enjoy it too.)

When I called Mr. G _____ to thank him, he told me that Grancy had finished the simple model with no trouble. He was amazed that Roosevelt was able to make a good start on the more difficult model (the one he wasn't planning on using). Mr. G _____ had asked Roosevelt if he had done any models before, and was told that the boy had done some with his big brother. Roosevelt asked Mr. G _____ if he might take the unfinished model home to finish it with his brother, and he was allowed to do it.

---

*Norman and Madelyn Carlisle, *The True Book of Automobiles* (Chicago: Childrens Press, 1965).

† Bradley Sussman, Northbrook, Ill.

Monday, November 22, 19--

After school, the boys and I walked over to the service station, and I introduced them to the owner. He brought us into the shop and asked the mechanics to show us what they were doing. We watched one man work on a tire. Then another mechanic lifted the hood on a car, showed us the parts inside and described their functions. He also lifted the car with a machine and showed us the parts underneath. After that we watched him work on brakes. Before then I never knew how they worked. We thanked everyone and left, talking about what we had seen. The boys told me that they had learned a lot. I know that I did.

MUSEUM TRIPS

On the way to the Museum of Science and Industry, I asked Roosevelt about the model car he took home, and he proudly told me that he finished it *without* his brother. I got the name of it, so I could tell Bradley not to buy the same one.

We used our Floor Plan to find the "Hall of Elements," and arrived just in time for a live chemistry demonstration. Using liquid nitrogen, a man demonstrated the following things:

He froze a rubber tube.

He froze a fresh flower until it was very hard, and then he made a powder of it.

He placed a rubber ball in the liquid nitrogen and the air pressure caved it in. The ball was very hard when he hit it on the table.

He froze an apple until it was very hard, and when he bounced it, it made a loud noise. Then he used the hard apple to drive a nail into balsa wood.

With the help of a girl from the audience, the demonstrator changed the chemical energy of perspiration into electricity, and he measured it on a galvanometer. Then he measured the electricity he got from the citric acid in an orange.

He showed other interesting things too. In one demonstration he combined some elements to make Styrofoam plastic — the kind used for insulation. We really enjoyed the chemistry demonstration!

Then we quickly toured the rest of the chemistry exhibits, most of which were too difficult. The children liked seeing the symbols that were used as "nicknames" for the various elements.

We made an unscheduled stop at an incubator for baby chicks, and watched one trying to get out of the egg. (This is one of my favorite exhibits.) We decided that it would take the chick a long time to come out, so we planned a return visit before we left. While we were there we also visited baby farm animals.

By then it was time for lunch and a rest. There were some good exhibits of prehistoric animals near the lunchroom, so we saw them on the way out. We viewed the fossils of early bone tools found in Africa, and then went on to see stone tools and modern machine tools. The guide at the "Chemical Man" film warned me that it would be too difficult for the children, so we didn't stop for it.

Then we went on to a special exhibit called "Motorama," where we saw the simple machines demonstrated, and we viewed a film clip history of automobiles, done with music and narration. We saw many early automobiles and other early vehicles.

With our remaining time we went through a model of the human heart. After that, we returned to the baby chick that had just emerged from the shell. It was exhausted, and it was wet and shaking.

On the way back we had a lot to talk about.

Monday, November 29, 19--

I went to the library to look for material in their picture and pamphlet files, and found nothing under "Collage," but I got pictures from "Art" and "Design." I looked fruitlessly under "Dinosaurs," "Cavemen," and "Prehistoric Times." Then I used the card catalog, and the cross reference card told me to look up "Animals — Prehistoric," where I found a whole stack of pictures. I got many pictures under "Automobiles," but none under "Cars" or "Motors."

The card catalog showed nothing on "Chemistry" for Roosevelt, so I checked a special Career File, which had some pamphlets which were too difficult.

Tuesday, November 30, 19--

I gave the overhead projector material on dinosaurs to Mitch and Gail, asking them to read it carefully. I'll give them the crossword puzzles and other lessons later.*

The children were very excited with the pictures from the library, and they all shared them.

After school, I made arrangements for a trip to The Art Institute to see collages.†

Friday, December 3, 19--

After I returned some materials to the library, I received a call from a young man, referred by the Volunteer Bureau, who is going to come in to work with the children on chemistry experiments. He wants me to plan the experiments and provide the supplies.

Monday, December 6, 19--

All of the trip slips, except Roosevelt's, are in for the rest of the trips. I phoned his mother, who said she didn't receive it, but she promised to send a note for Tuesday's trip.

Tuesday, December 7, 19--

I arrived at school loaded with racing car magazines that I gave to Roosevelt and Grancy to share. Roosevelt gave me the signed trip slip and said that his mother had found it. I finally turned in the trip slips that cover all the future expeditions. Thank goodness I'm done with them.

When we arrived at the Field Museum we toured the room that has prehistoric reptiles. We stayed with a guide for a while, but her vocabulary was too difficult for third graders, so we began our own tour, which was more fun. I used the question sheet called "Treasure Hunt," and followed it from exhibit to exhibit, asking questions about prehistoric reptiles and checking the children's answers. They did very well with it.

---

*See footnote, page 177 (Prehistoric Life).

†The Art Institute of Chicago, S. Michigan Ave. and E. Adams St., Chicago, Ill.

After lunch we walked through the "Egypt" room and saw the mummies and the Rosetta Stone replica. Then we found the room that had exhibits on prehistoric man. The children were fascinated by Cro-Magnon man's art work.

We took a rest and looked at the exhibits on Indians. By then the children said they were tired, so we headed back.

When I left the school I kept thinking about what Gail had said at the museum. "I'm going to take *my* children here a lot."

Thursday, December 9, 19--

I phoned Mr. G _____ to make sure he was coming, and we agreed to meet in the school office.

Mr. G _____ gave an interesting talk on "Dinosaurs" to two classes, and he showed pictures and answered questions. Then he stayed and we all watched the film about dinosaurs.* It was well done, showing moving models of the animals and an erupting volcano. The vocabulary used was a bit difficult in parts of the film, with such words as "inadequate." However, because it had so much action, the children enjoyed it.

The children wrote thank you letters to Mr. G _____. I sent one too, and I included a check to cover the cost of the two model cars.

I went to a library and returned some overdue books and reported a book that Roosevelt had lost. The librarian told me that it had been found on a bus and returned to a library in another suburb. She asked me to go there to get it, and when I drove there later they didn't have it. They claim it was probably sent back to my own local library. I called them and it wasn't there, but I'll try again.

Friday, December 10, 19--

I took care of many details today. I sent a note thanking the owner of the service station. Then I phoned the library about the lost book, found that it had been returned and informed Roosevelt's mother. I called Bradley about his visit, and reminded him to buy a model car.

---

*See footnote, page 178.

Monday, December 13, 19--

I briefed Bradley about Grancy and Roosevelt's abilities, and urged him to allow them to do as much on their own as possible. I arranged for them to use the Art Workshop, got some sandpaper ready and showed Bradley where to work.

He met the two boys, and they all had a great time assembling the model. Grancy will get to keep this model, because Roosevelt got the first big one. Grancy is keeping it at school until he gives his report. He also wants to show the class the book of antique cars, and some of his library pictures.

Roosevelt and I spoke briefly about what experiments he wants to do for his report. He plans to show the carbon dioxide one he tried out at home, in which a cork on a test tube is forced off by the "explosion" of carbon dioxide formed when he mixes baking soda and vinegar in the test tube. I promised to have test tubes, covers, a test tube stand, baking soda and vinegar for that day. He said he would try to bring a cork.

Bradley and I got the test tubes and covers, vinegar and a few other chemistry supplies ready, some for the experiments with Mr. M _____.

When I got home I wrote a thank you note to Bradley and his parents. It was an interesting morning.

KEYS TO LEARNING FROM PAST ERRORS
— SUMMING UP

Tuesday, December 14, 19--

When we arrived at The Art Institute,* we looked first at collages. One collage was made from railroad tickets written in German, and another had French writing on a piece of old newspaper. Some were construction paper designs and one, which was titled "Hey Valentine," had a piece of a valentine on it. We used a magnifying glass to examine the detail on the collages, and the children were fascinated.

---

*The Art Institute of Chicago, S. Michigan Ave. and E. Adams St., Chicago, Ill.

We saw modern paintings and sculpture and some very old Oriental sculpture.

Then it was time to go to the Junior Museum. It had a great exhibit called "Faces," in which the artistic possibilities of human faces were explored, using various media including paintings, masks, photographs and cut up mirrors. We visited a special room called the Rainbow Gallery for an exhibit and a recorded talk about color.

On the way home we discussed the children's reports very casually, planning what materials they would need from me. The youngsters are not writing anything out to read aloud. I suggested that they plan what they're going to do, and if they wish, write down a short list of what they're going to tell about. In this way we will try to avoid the nervousness that memorizing could cause them; and also avoid their reading aloud in a boring way. The children know that they will meet with me afterward to discuss the reports.

That evening I phoned Mr. M _____to verify Wednesday's visit, and I told him that all of the supplies and books were ready.

Wednesday, December 15, 19--

Early in the morning I made arrangements for a big formica table for Mr. M _____. His visit went very well, and the children were all interested.

Later, I wrote thank you notes to Mr. M _____and to the Volunteer Bureau of Evanston.

Thursday, December 16, 19--

Today was the last day of our project. I brought in the book of antique cars, the collage book and some chemistry supplies for the reports. I had some large test tubes with covers in case Roosevelt didn't bring a cork.

The children were keyed up about their reports. Some nervousness showed in their voices, which could barely be heard. Otherwise, they appeared to be very relaxed.

Mitch showed pictures of prehistoric animals. He also answered some questions from the class.

Grancy and I displayed the book of antique cars, (it was heavy to hold) and I also helped him read a few names. Then he showed the model he had made with Bradley. Grancy spoke in a very animated way about the trip to the service station and the brake shoes. I had never heard him talk so much.

Pam displayed her collages, and told about some of the materials she used. She also showed my old book of one hundred collages.

Gail exhibited some dinosaur pictures from the school library, and then her collages.

Roosevelt came last. He attempted the carbon dioxide experiment he had practiced at home. He had forgotten the cork, so we used a large test tube with a cover. I helped by holding the test tube, which was too large for the wooden holder. Roosevelt put baking soda and vinegar in the tube and tried to cover it before the carbon dioxide fizzed up. The first time he was too late, so he tried it again in another test tube. There didn't seem to be enough vinegar or baking soda then, and I asked the class what they thought we should do. They all agreed we should add more vinegar and baking soda, so Roosevelt did that. This time there was enough baking soda and vinegar, and he got the cover on in time (with a little help), but the cover wasn't popped off by the forming carbon dioxide. We talked it over, and I asked Roosevelt what he wanted to do. He said that since he had used a cork at home, he thought he should do it with a cork. We both said that we would try hard to get one, so that he could do the experiment again. Roosevelt promised to clean up the table and test tubes.

I met with my group for a short evaluation session, using the same forms that I used with the first project group. (See Figure 8-3.)

Some comments about Mitch's report:

WHAT I LIKED ABOUT THE REPORT *I liked it very much.*

I THINK THE REPORT COULD HAVE BEEN EVEN BETTER BY *talking lowder*

About Pam's report:

WHAT I LIKED ABOUT THE REPORT *I liked the collage.*

WHAT I LIKED ABOUT THE REPORT *I liked Mrs Ashlys book of collages.*

I THINK THE REPORT COULD HAVE BEEN EVEN BETTER BY *she did not talk loud anofe.*

About Grancy's report:

WHAT I LIKED ABOUT THE REPORT *I liked the model. I liked the book.*

I THINK THE REPORT COULD HAVE BEEN EVEN BETTER BY *he could maked it mor longer*

Some comments about Gail's report:

WHAT I LIKED ABOUT THE REPORT *the neat pictures*

WHAT I LIKED ABOUT THE REPORT *everything*

WHAT I LIKED ABOUT THE REPORT *it was grate*

I THINK THE REPORT COULD HAVE BEEN EVEN BETTER BY *a little more pictures   louder*

I THINK THE REPORT COULD HAVE BEEN EVEN BETTER BY *a collage on dinosaurs (Gail's own comment)*

About Roosevelt's report:

WHAT I LIKED ABOUT THE REPORT *everything*

WHAT I LIKED ABOUT THE REPORT *the experment*

WHAT I LIKED ABOUT THE REPORT *that was real cool*

I THINK THE REPORT COULD HAVE BEEN EVEN BETTER BY *a cork (Roosevelt's own comment)*

I THINK THE REPORT COULD HAVE BEEN EVEN BETTER BY *I dont think anything could of been impruved*

An interesting thing: nearly each child noticed that the others couldn't be heard well, and they had all heard me ask them to speak louder. Yet, each one spoke very softly himself.

I couldn't collect all of the library's pictures, because Grancy had forgotten to bring his, so I suggested that we display them until the next day, when I would collect everything. I put a reminder note in Grancy's pocket.

To sum up, we spoke about what the children had learned for making future reports. Everyone in the group agreed that he or she should speak louder. Roosevelt decided that he shouldn't do an experiment for the group until he has the correct equipment that he practiced with.

I concluded the meeting by saying that there were only a few things that could have been improved. I said that I was very proud of their fine reports, and that the other children had liked them too. The youngsters were quite pleased with themselves.

Later, Roosevelt and I searched a long time for a cork in the Science Supply room, and we finally found one.

That evening I phoned Grancy's mother to ask her to send the pictures with him the next day, as this would be the last chance before vacation.

Friday, December 17, 19--

Roosevelt did his experiment successfully, and everyone cheered. It was fun.

I collected all of the pictures and books — thank goodness!

And now it was over. I think that the children in my special group got a lot out of it. I know that I was enriched.

As you can see, all enrichment groups differ in many ways. Everything is open-ended, and preparation must wait until the pupils select their topics.

HOW TO BEGIN YOUR OWN
INDIVIDUALIZED ENRICHMENT PROJECTS

A great deal of time and telephoning may be needed for a small individual enrichment group in which each student selects his own subject, especially if you go on many trips and use the services of volunteer talent. However, you will feel that it was very worthwhile.

In case you live in an area where there are few or no museums, organized nature centers and other places of that type to visit, you can make fewer trips and still have fine projects. Your own area may have other places of interest to visit: for example, forests, cliffs, farms or factories. Nearly every town has a park, a library, a service station and interesting rock formations or road cuts for highways. Children can be enriched by studying landforms, rocks, plants, animals, lumber mills, brickyards and how to make things anywhere.

Volunteer talent may not be as organized in small cities and towns as they are in many big cities. But, wherever there are people, you will find talent and willingness to help if you look for it and ask for it.

There are several good ways to have enrichment groups other than the small group method taught by one teacher within a self-contained classroom. A school can hire a special teacher for two mornings a week, or a principal can conduct such a group. A team of two teachers can arrange their groupings so that one teacher is free to work with a small group a few times a week while the other one works with the large group. This could easily be done by showing films or filmstrips for the large group and having discussions about them. The field trips in this case could be shared by the two classes and it would cut the expense of the bus. Student teachers or volunteers could also be used for special enrichment groups and the entire class could share the trips with them.

It is not usually necessary to buy extra supplies, because time and effort are the big requirements. You may need to buy something special in case a child chooses a topic that is not usually taught in the school; or when you do not know enough about the subject; or when you cannot find enough materials.

With planning, you can meet successfully with your small group and still keep the rest of the class constructively busy on their regular assignments. Handwriting practice, dictionary work, spelling practice, free reading, art work and map work are only a few possibilities of valuable extra work that can be planned in case your class finishes its assignment before you and your group are ready to join them.

The rest of your class will be very cooperative while you work with your enrichment group, because they know that they will also have a turn for a special project.

Good communication is vital to your success, and first of all, you need rapport with the children. The other teachers who may be involved — the principal, the librarian and sometimes the parents — must be contacted in a tactful way. Keep the channels open and friendly with the child's other teachers, if he has them.

Strive for a balance between not doing enough in the child's field of interest and between doing too much, so that he does not lose valuable instruction or practice in his regular lessons.

In any case, the main ingredient for success is the leader's enthusiasm. The more freedom the children have to follow their own (and each other's) interests, the more successful the project will be.

Good luck with whatever extra you can do for all of your children. There will never be enough. Just remember that if special opportunities are provided for individual enrichment, the excitement and interest will spread and you'll find that you have provided a great deal of enrichment for *all.*

CHECKLIST

* Allow pupils to switch topics at the beginning of the project, if they wish to.
* Plan carefully for individualized enrichment projects to motivate and expand the students' interests.
* Schedule trips and volunteer speakers as far in advance as you can.
* Ask your school librarian for suggestions and help.
* Use real experiences in the chosen topics whenever possible.
* Try to find different *kinds* of audio-visual enrichment materials.
* Talk to people about your enrichment groups, and they will offer help and materials.
* Help pupils plan their reports, and check that they have all necessary supplies ahead of time.
* Invest your time in planning trips and guest speakers for the learning, variety and stimulation they will give.
* Explore the resources of your own area for enrichment possibilities.
* Communicate clearly and tactfully with everyone concerned.
* Be enthused about each child's projects, because your enthusiasm will be contagious.

10

Individualizing Instruction with Self-Checking and Programmed Materials

Good teaching requires some self-checking materials so that pupils may work at their own pace on their individual interests. Because the checking reinforces learning, it is a vital part of the process. Self-checking satisfies, corrects, rewards, punishes and motivates.

All programmed materials are self-checking, but for a lesson to be considered programmed, it must be a planned progression of small steps leading to the learning of at least one concept or fact.

This chapter will tell you how to use tapes, answer sheets and teachers' manuals for self-checking, and it will discuss the merits and disadvantages of these methods. It will help you to plan the best programmed instruction for each child, and it will suggest easy ways to keep individual records that will satisfy your students' needs for goals and evaluation. Examples of various types of good self-checking and programmed materials are also provided.

SELF-CHECKING WITH TAPES

Use a tape recorder to help students check their own work when they need it. It will not be necessary to keep the tape recorder in your classroom at all times if it must be borrowed, as you may wish to sign up for a recorder for an hour a day, and just keep your own self-checking tape.

Tape-recorded answers or lessons can effectively check most kinds of student work with the exception of spelling and handwriting, which are done best visually. You may even use a tape for a self-evaluation on creative writing. The following suggested message can be used for middle and upper grade students:

Read through your first paragraph or sentence to see if it makes sense and provides a good beginning. Please stop the tape and start it again when you're ready....

Now, read through each sentence to see whether it says what you intended and whether you have complete sentences or just parts of sentences. Take the time to make changes if you need them. Stop the tape and start again when you're ready...

Check each sentence for punctuation and capitals. Do you have periods, commas and question marks where you need them? If not, write them in when you stop the tape. Start it again when you're ready...

Look through your writing to see whether all the spelling looks correct to you. If a word looks as if it may be incorrectly spelled, please circle it for checking with the dictionary later. Stop the tape and start it again when you're ready...

Read through your last paragraph or ending. Does it give a good finish to your composition? Change it if you can improve it. Stop the tape and start it again when you're ready...

Now you're almost finished. Read through your work from the beginning to the end without stopping. Does it say what you would like it to say to your reader? Can you change it in a way to say it even better? If you can think of a better word or way of putting your sentences together, try to improve your writing. Stop the tape and start it again when you're ready...

Now — stop the tape and use a dictionary to look up and correct all the circled words that may have been incorrectly spelled. Start the tape again when you're ready...

If you have the time, stop the tape here, put your creative writing away, and start the tape at this place tomorrow, after you read your work to see if you can make it even better. You may want to say something in a different way, or you may have new ideas that you want to add. If you don't have time, please go on.

Before you hand in your writing to your teacher, please recopy it neatly in your best handwriting. Turn off the tape recorder.

Another kind of self-checking tape could contain the following answers for mathematics:

Chapter 1. Page 1. Problem 1. 4-3/4. Problem 2. 7-1/2. Problem 3. 4-7/8. Page 4. Problem 1. 12-5/6. Problem 2. 7-1/3. Problem 3. 56-9/10 ...

This type of tape could easily be recorded by student helpers. However, in all cases, it would be necessary to have the answer tape checked, and other students could do this.

Students will tire of any self-checking method, so try to vary the tapes with other kinds of self-checking; for example, visual methods that use books or answer sheets.

PROVIDING YOUR OWN ANSWER SHEETS FOR SELF-CHECKING — PROS AND CONS

One of the simplest kinds of self-checking is to have pupils use answer sheets that you write, type or copy yourself. This kind can be duplicated and cut into strips. When clipped together into groups arranged by page numbers, these answer sheets can be used by individuals for any kind of lesson that has an objective answer. Some examples are given below:

P. 21	P. 40	P. 193
1.) 46	1.) Pacific	1.) either
2.) 29	2.) Atlantic	2.) neither
3.) 78	3.) Mediterranean	3.) neighbor
4.) 81	4.) Indian	4.) sleigh
5.) 114	5.) Aegean	5.) weigh

These short answer sheets can be very useful because they are small units and can be used as needed. They are easily portable and can function anywhere, even for outdoor lessons, when clipped in piles. They provide a visual reinforcement that is essential for checking spelling practice.

The disadvantages of using the teacher-prepared answer sheets are the time and effort needed to prepare them. Also, some children cheat with answer sheets at times, but in most cases this type of self-checking is useful. If many different texts and lessons are being used in one class, it may not be worth the time needed for writing or typing and cutting so many of them. If you have access to a copying machine it may be efficient to copy answers, duplicate and cut them into strips. However, many textbooks have problems scattered in a way that would make this type of copying difficult.

Written answer sheets will be most useful if they can be purchased or copied for duplication, if they can be used for more than one school year and if they can be shared with other teachers.

They may be considered an investment of time and energy that will yield profits in student motivation and learning and teacher marking time. Although the checked pupil work should be skimmed later, answer sheets save the teacher a great deal of marking time. The children are able to check their progress as they work, and this makes their lessons more important to them.

MAKING USE OF TEACHERS' MANUALS

Of course, there are excellent ideas for lessons and supplementary activities in most teachers' copies of textbooks. Another way to make use of teachers' manuals is to use them for self-checking purposes for students who are working on their own. You may possibly borrow an extra copy or two for an hour from the library or from another teacher. I have found teachers' editions of workbooks to be valuable self-checking resources, and they are inexpensive in case you want to order an extra copy.

Children can take turns checking their own workbooks in this way, preferably after each page is completed. Since the class will probably be using many reading series and levels, this can be a practical way to provide checking while it is most meaningful to the student.

EFFECTIVE LEARNING ACTIVITIES

One of the most effective, newer linguistic approaches to primary reading instruction is *Plays for Echo Reading.** It relates reading to speech and provides a model for standard speech patterns.

---

*Donald D. Durrell and Lorraine A. DeMilia, *Plays for Echo Reading* (New York: Harcourt, Brace & World, Inc., 1970).

This boxed set contains twelve copies of pupils' books, eight LP 33-1/3 RPM twelve-inch records on which more than half of the plays are recorded, along with directions to the pupils for use in echo-reading sessions and a teacher's manual.

Children work in groups of two. After a child listens to a play read aloud by superior readers, he hears the lines of the play read separately as he follows the printed text. He then echoes the dramatic expression. After two such practices, he and his partner read the play aloud, using the lively expression presented on the record. After this independent practice, the various drama teams can combine for a choral reading of the play.

Echo reading helps children develop expressive oral reading, increase phrase perception, acquire more rapid and accurate word recognition, expand their reading vocabulary and increase their reading achievement.

A very useful supplementary mathematics program for grades four through six can individualize instruction.* This forty tape series is correlated with current basic mathematics textbooks, and it can reinforce and extend mathematics concepts. Each tape has an accompanying pupil response booklet and is a self-directed lesson.

Learning to Use a Globe, which is part of a *Globe Skills Kit,* will help to teach global concepts in the early school years.† It is designed for individual or group study, and pupils can check their own work with answers provided on the backs of cards.

Another interesting teaching tool is *Map & Globe Skills,*‡ part of the SRA Basic Skills Series for grades four through six. Once the introductory lesson has been given by the teacher, the pupil proceeds independently as rapidly as he is able within each unit. The child practices skills by doing exercises presented on skill cards. He corrects work by means of key cards and keeps a record

---

*Dr. Lola J. May, *Intermediate Math Program,* Imperial International Learning Corporation, Kankakee, Ill. 60901.

† Parmer L. Ewing and Marion H. Seibel, *Learning to Use a Globe,* Set I, *Globe Skills Kit,* No. GK100. A.J. Nystrom & Co., Chicago, Ill. 60618, A subsidiary of Field Enterprises, Inc.

‡ Robert A. Naslund and Charles M. Brown, *Map & Globe Skills,* MG II, SRA Basic Skills Series, Science Research Associates, Inc., 259 E. Erie St., Chicago, Ill. 60611. 1964.

of his progress. Multiple learning experiences are provided at each level of difficulty.

EXAMPLES OF VARIOUS TYPES OF
PROGRAMMED LEARNING

You will enjoy the rich variety of programmed learning materials. However, they can become too impersonal unless you keep in close touch with the learners; helping, encouraging, praising and checking them.

The System 80 teaching machines are fascinating to see and work with. Pupils enjoy the colorful lessons and the novelty of working with a machine.

When the learner answers a question correctly, the machine directs him to the next question. If the answer is incorrect, the question is repeated and rephrased.

Developing Spelling Skills, Kit A,* is an example.

Beginning with Kit A, the child takes the placement test (or pretest). This test will prescribe only those lessons in the kit he needs. The lesson jacket contains a record and filmslide having eighty synchronized full-color visual and audio messages. The filmslide has two sides, each side corresponding to a side of the record. The lesson jacket also contains a prescription key (a scoring card that the teacher will use to plan the child's work).

In all levels, side one is used as a pretest and side two is the post-test. A group-administered prescription test for each kit is also available for pretesting the entire class at one time. The test package includes duplicating masters.

Each day the student refers to his student record card in the student record book (kept with the audio-visual unit and lessons).

He identifies his lesson for the day by finding the first circled number on the card which has not been crossed out. (The student marks an X through each prescribed lesson that he has completed.)

The student removes the appropriate lesson jacket from the kit. The record and filmslide are inserted into the audio-visual unit and the lesson proceeds in the same manner as the pretest.

---

* *Developing Spelling Skills,* Kit A, No. 2041, System 80, Borg-Warner Educational Systems, A Division of Borg-Warner Corporation, Chicago, Ill. 60604. 1969.

If a student requires work in any lesson he must also take the appropriate review lesson and have the Student Record Card marked accordingly. Each kit has two review lessons which cover the words presented. Because of the branching* technique used in this review lesson, two separate review patterns are possible:

1. a challenging review sequence for the student who has mastered the preceding lessons.

2. a remedial sequence for the student who needs additional practice on the material presented in the preceding lessons.

Some learning kits can be considered programmed materials. One called *Skill Modes in Mathematics* has twenty-six major computational skills called molecules.† Each molecule is sub-divided into learning tasks, or atoms. Skill cards are the core of the program, and each atom is the basis of a skill card.

A student succeeds on part *a* of a skill card by getting eighty percent of the problems correct. If he succeeds, he gets a choice. He can go on to the next skill card, or he can skip a few cards and do one that's harder. If he doesn't succeed, he works parts *b* and *c*, — the prerequisites. If he still has trouble, he is sent to the Stop and Think cards for any prerequisite where he needs help. He also works a Stop and Think card for the atom he started with. Then he comes back to complete part *d* of the atom he began with. If he is now successful (by getting eighty percent correct), he goes on to a new skill card. Answers are on the reverse side of cards.

Stop and Think cards are the instructional mode of the program, and there's one for each atom. The front of each of these cards contains a simple explanation with drawings or an example, and the back has a set of programmed-practice problems.

The third type of card is a practice card. These cards review a series of atoms, and they recycle the student through the Stop

---

*Selection of next lesson depends on response given in current lesson.

†Dr. Robert Gagne, Sr. Elinor Ford, Dr. M. Vere De Vault and Veronica Berreen, *Skill Modes in Mathematics*, Level 1, No. 3-44010, Science Research Associates, Inc., 259 E. Erie St., Chicago, Ill. 60611. 1974.

and Think cards related to any errors he makes. You can use the practice cards for diagnosis. They refer you to specific Stop and Think and skill cards for necessary reteaching.

The Student Record book contains skill charts that enable the student to keep a record of where he is and how he is progressing. Survey and Mastery tests diagnose and evaluate. The Survey tests specify, by problem, the exact skills to be studied, and the Mastery Tests indicate overall achievement and any specific areas in which a student needs to be recycled through a skill sequence.

Another type of programmed learning that also controls the student's access to and through the material and gives continuous and immediate evaluation of the student's program is scrambled programming. An example of a scrambled intrinsic programmed booklet is provided for you in Chapter Eleven.

The booklet is a single concept teaching tool. In each program step the pupil is given material to read, which is followed by a multiple-choice question. The pupil's answer choice determines directly and automatically what he will see next by sending him to a specific page which is presented in scrambled order in the booklet. If he chooses the correct answer to the question, he is directed to the next paragraph or sentence of material and the next question. If he chooses an incorrect answer, he is presented with a paragraph written specifically to correct the particular error he has just made. At the end of this correctional material the student will be directed to return to the original presentation to try the original question again, or he will be branched to a sub-sequence of instructional text and questions in which the originally troublesome point is explained with a different approach or in smaller, simpler steps. This type of program automatically adapts to individual differences among pupils.

PLANNING THE BEST PROGRAMMED
INSTRUCTION FOR EACH INDIVIDUAL

Availability of materials will limit your planning to a great degree. Many types of programmed instruction are expensive and, therefore, difficult to obtain.

Plan ahead for obtaining programmed learning materials

from your Learning Center. Reserve kits and teaching machines that are not available when you ask for them.

Borrow what you can, and study the programmed teaching tools on the market before you purchase one. Look for materials that will be useful for many children in your group, not just for two or three. Try to have some programmed learning for teaching new concepts and some for practicing skills.

Use large group instruction for introducing a new teaching machine or learning kit to your class. Then, work with small groups or individuals as they begin to use the materials. Make sure that they understand the complete procedure before the children begin to work on their own. Help them with the self-checking and recording of progress the first time, and then they will enjoy and use the programs.

Pupils who are having reading difficulties will learn well with teaching machines or sets that have a record or cassette as well as skill cards or books. Encourage restless children to take short breaks as they work on their own, and they will accomplish a great deal more. Ask those who get easily bored to come up and show you how they are doing once in a while. A short walk and some interest and approval from you will really keep them going.

EASY RECORD-KEEPING THAT SATISFIES STUDENTS' NEEDS FOR GOALS AND EVALUATION

You will probably want to keep at least three kinds of simple records: a class grade book, a small diagnostic notebook for each child (described in Chapters One and Two) and the records that the children fill out on their own.

An example of a student's progress record sheet on programmed language booklets could be:

PROGRAMMED BOOKLETS				
			(7 questions)	
Title	Started	Finished	Pretest	Post-test
Freddy and the Subject	5-1-__	5-2-__	+2	+7
Freddy and the Predicate	5-2-__		+1	

Figure 10-1

Expect students to keep progress charts on their own independent work, whether they are using teaching machines, learning kits or programmed booklets. If there is no progress chart provided for individuals, have each student keep a separate notebook page for each project to chart progress in his work. The simple notations would include the name of the project, telling whether it was an independent research project, an experiment or a single concept booklet; the date started and the date completed; and in some cases, the score on the activity if it includes a post-test or a quiz.

All individuals of any age need a sense of purpose and accomplishment; and the progress charts of all kinds fill this need by recording the work completed, as well as scores. Many of the printed progress charts show the remaining skill cards, lessons or booklets yet to be done. They help to set goals for the student and give him motivation to keep working, as well as provide evaluation of his efforts.

CHECKLIST

* Reinforce learning by having students check their own work.
* Tape record answers or checklists so that students can evaluate and mark on their own.
* Use some answer sheets for immediate pupil checking, and skim the work later.
* Have students check their work with teachers' manuals and teachers' editions of workbooks.
* Relate reading to speech and provide a model for standard speech patterns by using recorded plays and echo reading.
* Make use of the programmed materials available to you: machines, kits or booklets.
* Help students to become familiar with programmed learning procedures before they work independently.
* See that pupils with reading problems work independently with audio-visual materials rather than with those that are just visual.
* Write some of your own programmed lesson booklets to fit your pupils' specific needs.
* Keep individual diagnostic notebooks for each child.
* Require independent record-keeping of progress charts from each student in order to satisfy his need for goals and evaluation.

Sample Plan for a Programmed Lesson Booklet

You can use programmed materials to teach any concept or any subject, if these teaching tools are available. They add variety to your other teaching methods. Chapter Ten describes some commercially-prepared programmed instruction that you may wish to use.

This chapter contains material for you to utilize to make a sample programmed booklet in the scrambled style. Each booklet page is separated by lines. The lessons in the booklet contain multiple-choice questions. The pupil's choice of an answer guides him to his next lesson.

The objectives for this booklet are:

Pupils can correctly identify:

1) a real sentence

2) the function of a predicate in a simple sentence

3) the location of a predicate in a simple sentence

4) a predicate in a simple sentence

If you find that this plan for a programmed lesson booklet could be useful to you, copy it on a dittomaster and run off enough copies for all of your pupils who would benefit from them. The book *Activities for Motivating and Teaching Bright Children** has a plan for another similar booklet called "Freddy and the Subject,"

---

*Rosalind Minor Ashley, *Activities for Motivating and Teaching Bright Children* (West Nyack, N.Y.: Parker Publishing Co., Inc., 1973), pp. 37-74.

as well as a chapter that will help you to write programmed booklets to teach anything you wish. By writing your own scrambled booklets you can teach concepts needed by individuals in your group, and you can control the reading level and vocabulary in order to have materials for the very slowest and also for those who need the most challenge.

Whenever you assign scrambled programmed booklets, use their pretests — post-tests first to make sure that the pupils need to learn the programmed material. An example of this type of test is given in Chapter One.

If the child earns a score of less than six out of a possible seven points on this test, record the pretest score and assign the booklet. If he earns six or seven on the test, record the score and skip the booklet, allowing him to go on to more advanced work. A sample record page for recording scores on programmed booklets is given in Chapter Ten.

If the pupil needs to be branched to remedial work or has time for enrichment work, help him to get started with the appropriate materials suggested at the end of the programmed booklet. Substitute similar work if these books and workbooks are not available.

When the child has completed the programmed booklet and any extra work on it, give him a fresh copy of the test and have him take it again. After marking the post-test with the pupil, give the marked test back to him so that he can see his score and learn the correct answers for the questions he missed.

If the child misses more than one answer on the post-test, direct him to other media which teach the same concept. Look for records, filmstrips or tapes. Do not repeat the booklet. This is probably a good time for an individual conference to reteach and encourage.

A perfect score or one error on the post-test can be considered good enough for the pupil to go on to another programmed booklet.

Freddy and the Predicate

Figure 11-1

Freddy: Hi, Professor Bumble. Sorry I'm late.

Prof. B.: All right, Freddy. But, don't do it again. I hope that you can sit still today.

Freddy: Oh, sure.

Prof. B.: Do you remember how to use these booklets?

Freddy: Yeah. I choose the best answer, and that tells me what page to turn to.

Prof. B.: Good. Right now, please turn to Page 30.

Prof. B.: I think you're tired now, Freddy. You'll work on this again tomorrow with a special *R* book and workbook,

and your teacher will help you with it. Go tell her about
it right now. Good-by.

Page 3

Freddy: We sure hop around this booklet.

Prof. B.: You should like that.

Freddy: I do.

Prof. B.: Choose the best answer from the next group. You are to
select the sentence with the predicate missing.
(a)   Boys and girls like to play ball. (Turn to Page 10.)
(b)   Boys and girls like to play. (Turn to Page 10.)
(c)   Boys like to play ball. (Turn to Page 10.)
(d)   Boys and girls. (Turn to Page 4.)

Page 4

Freddy: Did I do it?

Prof. B.: You sure did. Your sentence has a subject, but the predicate is missing. Well done. Turn to Page 8.

Page 5

Freddy: Did I do it again?

Prof. B.: Yes. I'm afraid so. What is a predicate, Freddy?

Freddy: The end?

Prof. B.: Yes. You know it. It's the end of a simple sentence that
tells what the subject *does,* or tells something about it.

Freddy: I gave the whole sentence, didn't I?

Prof. B.: Yup.

Freddy: And I was supposed to choose the one with the predicate *missing?*

Prof. B.: Yup. Try again. Turn to Page 8.

Page 6

Prof. B.: Choose the sentence with the entire last part missing.
  (a) Men and women play golf. (Turn to Page 22.)
  (b) Men play golf. (Turn to Page 22.)
  (c) Men and women. (Turn to Page 18.)

Page 7

Prof. B.: Your answer was the subject of a sentence. Do you remember what a subject is?

Freddy: I'm not sure.

Prof. B.: The subject is the first part of a simple sentence.

Freddy: Oh, yeah.

Prof. B.: Do you remember what it does in a sentence?

Freddy: Uh. It tells who she is.

Prof. B.: I think you've got it. The subject tells *who* or *what* does something, or is being talked about.

Freddy: Oh.

Prof. B.: But, this answer wasn't correct, because it was only part of a sentence — the first part. Please turn to Page 11.

Page 8

Prof. B.: Let's try another sentence. Select the one sentence with the predicate missing.
  (a) Houses can be made of brick or wood. (Turn to Page 5.)
  (b) Houses. (Turn to Page 14.)
  (c) Houses can be made of brick. (Turn to Page 5.)
  (d) Can be made of brick or wood. (Turn to Page 17.)

Page 9

Freddy: Well, here I am.

Prof. B.: Congratulations. You're correct on the first one.

Freddy: Yeah! Yeah!

Prof. B.: O. K. Settle down. We can't celebrate this soon. Now that you know what a real sentence is, we can go on to talk about its parts. Do you remember what a subject is?

Freddy: Sort of. It's who she is.

Prof. B.: Well, yes. The subject is the part of the sentence that tells you who or what it's about. For example, "The little girl."

Freddy: Oh, yeah.

Prof. B.: So, the subject is the first part of a simple sentence that tells who or what does something, or is being talked about. Please turn to Page 11.

Page 10

Freddy: Oh, oh. I have a feeling I did something wrong.

Prof. B.: Well, you chose a correct sentence, but that isn't what you were asked to do.

Freddy: Oh. That's what I did wrong. Let me try again.

Prof. B.: O. K. Turn back to Page 3 and choose the sentence with the predicate missing.

Page 11

Freddy: Here I am.

Prof. B.: If I say, "the little girl," do I tell you anything about her?

Freddy: Well, you tell me she's little.

Prof. B.: Right. But, after I say, "the little girl," aren't you waiting to hear something about her?

Freddy: Like what?

Prof. B.: Like what she's doing or thinking or feeling.

Freddy: Yeah.

Prof. B.: Or, I could say, "the girl is little," and then I'm telling something about the girl, and there's an end to the sentence. So, that's why the subject is only part of a real sentence. The end part is missing. Please turn to Page 13.

Page 12

Freddy: O. K. Here we are.

Prof. B.: In your sentence, "the bicycle" is what it's about.

Freddy: Right.

Prof. B.: The rest of your sentence tells what happened to the bicycle –"broke the little girl."

Freddy: That's silly.

Prof. B.: Sure it's silly. It's what we call a nonsense sentence. But, it's a real sentence, because it has a subject that tells what it's about. It also has a *predicate* that tells us something about the subject.

Freddy: Oh.

Prof. B.: We'll practice a lot more with predicates, Freddy, if you can keep from wiggling. I'm glad that you chose a real sentence. Please turn to Page 13.

Page 13

Prof. B.: So, the subject is the first part of a simple sentence that tells who or what it's about. What else does a sentence need?

Freddy: A period at the end.

Prof. B.: Yes, it does. But, what have we just been talking about that a sentence needs besides a subject?

Freddy: The other part. The end part. I don't remember.

Prof. B.: You got it! The end part that tells what the subject is doing. Very good!

Freddy: It is?

Prof. B.:   Yes. You know what a predicate does. You can easily learn its name — *predicate.*

Freddy: Predicate.

Prof. B.:   Right. Now, please turn to Page 3.

Page 14

Prof. B.:   You're getting sharper all the time, Freddy. This is the correct answer. "Houses" is the subject of the sentence, and the entire predicate is missing. The predicate is "can be made of brick or wood." It could also be "can be made of brick."

Freddy: I'm pretty good, ain't I?

Prof. B.:   Yes. You're doing fine. Turn to Page 6.

Page 15

Prof. B.:   I think you're playing tricks on me, Freddy. You know that (c) didn't make sense.

Freddy: I guess so. But, I don't remember what a real sentence is.

Prof. B.:   Well, we'll give you lots of practice in working on sentences. The first part of a simple sentence could be "The little girl." It tells who or what the sentence is about.

Freddy: Oh.

Prof. B.:   But, "The little girl" is only part of a sentence. It's the first part of a simple sentence that we call a *subject.* Please turn to Page 11.

Page 16

Prof. B.:   Well, Freddy. You were partly right.

Freddy: I was?

Prof. B.:   Yes. You chose a real sentence, but it didn't make sense. Remember that you were to select a sentence that made sense. "The bicycle" is the subject of your sentence. Do you remember what a subject is?

Freddy: I'm not sure.

Prof. B.: "The bicycle" is the subject of your sentence, and it tells who or what the sentence is about. Please turn to Page 12.

Page 17

Freddy: Did I do it wrong?

Prof. B.: Yes, Freddy. You chose the sentence with the *subject* missing. The predicate is there. "Can be made of brick or wood" tells about the houses, so it's a predicate. Let's try another one. Please turn to Page 6.

Page 18

Prof. B.: Good work, Freddy. You chose the answer with the last part missing.

Freddy: Is it time for lunch yet?

Prof. B.: Pretty soon, but not yet. Freddy, can you tell me a name for the last part of the simple sentence — the part that was missing? Choose it.
(a) Prejudice. (Turn to Page 20.)
(b) Subject (Turn to Page 19.)
(c) Predicate (Turn to Page 23.)

Page 19

Freddy: I can tell by the look on your face that I goofed.

Prof. B.: Well, we're just starting. Where does a subject come in a simple sentence, Freddy?

Freddy: At the start?

Prof. B.: Right. The subject starts a simple sentence, and it tells *who* or *what* it's about. Turn back to the question on Page 18 and choose the correct name for the last part of a simple sentence — the part that tells something about the subject.

Page 20

Prof. B.: I'm sorry, Freddy. I was being tricky. *Prejudice* sounds a lot like *predicate*. Maybe we should quit soon and finish later.

Freddy: I'm not tired, Professor. I was just sort of daydreaming.

Prof. B.: O. K. Freddy. Turn back to the question on Page 18 and choose the correct name for the last part of a simple sentence.

Page 21

Prof. B.: Well, we're getting there, Freddy. You chose *part* of the predicate.

Freddy: I lost some of it?

Prof. B.: Yes. The complete predicate is "are very brave." It includes everything but the subject.

Freddy: Oh.

Prof. B.: What is the subject of this sentence? It's on Page 23.

Freddy: Uh. Firemen?

Prof. B.: Right. Everything else in the sentence tells about the firemen, so it's called the *predicate*. Let's try one more. Turn to Page 24.

Page 22

Prof. B.: You aren't really concentrating, Freddy. Let's take a short break. Stretch up to the ceiling.

Freddy: I can jump up there.

Prof. B.: I know. But, let's just stretch right now.

Freddy: O. K.

Prof. B.: Do you know what answer you chose?

Freddy: The wrong one.

Prof. B.: Why was it incorrect?

Freddy: I'm not sure.

Prof. B.:   You were asked to choose a sentence with the last part missing, and you chose a complete sentence.

Freddy: Oh.

Prof. B.:   It had a subject, and it had a predicate.

Freddy: Oh.

Prof. B.:   Do you know what the predicate was?

Freddy: The end?

Prof. B.:   Yes. "Play golf." Please turn back to Page 6 and try again.

Page 23

Prof. B.:   Correct! Very good! Let's practice with predicates. Choose the sentence that has the entire predicate underlined.
    (a) Firemen <u>are very brave</u>. (Turn to Page 27.)
    (b) Firemen are <u>very brave.</u> (Turn to Page 21.)
    (c) <u>Firemen</u> are very brave. (Turn to Page 25.)

Page 24

Prof. B.:   Choose the sentence that has the whole predicate underlined.
    (a) <u>She</u> sat on the swing. (Turn to Page 26.)
    (b) She <u>sat</u> on the swing. (Turn to Page 29.)
    (c) She <u>sat on the swing</u>. (Turn to Page 28.)

Page 25

Freddy: Can I stand up now, Professor?

Prof. B.:   If you don't wiggle.

Freddy: O. K.

Prof. B.:   Your answer was "firemen." "Firemen" is the subject of the sentence. It tells who the sentence is about. A predicate is the last part of a simple sentence, and it tells what the firemen are doing, or what they're like. Let's try one more, Freddy. Please turn to Page 24.

Freddy: Wrong again?

Prof. B.:   I'm afraid so. You chose the sentence with the *subject* underlined. Let's try one more, Freddy. Remember, the predicate is the last part of a simple sentence, and it tells what the subject does or feels or looks like.

Freddy: O. K.

Prof. B.:   Choose the sentence with the whole predicate underlined.
            (a) The dog ran. (Turn to Page 2.)
            (b) The dog ran. (Turn to Page 2.)
            (c) The dog ran. (Turn to Page 31.)

Prof. B.:   I think I can let you eat lunch right now, Freddy. You're doing so well! You chose the sentence with the underlined predicate.

Freddy: Good.

Prof. B.:   What was the subject in that sentence? It's on Page 23.

Freddy: Let me look at it again. Uh. "Firemen"?

Prof. B.:   Great! Please ask your teacher for an *E*-1 book and workbook. She'll help you get started. Do at least three assigned workbook pages after all the reading. See you for your next booklet.

Prof. B.:   You've done very well, Freddy, and I think you understand what a predicate is. It's the last part of a simple sentence, and it tells what?

Freddy: About the subject.

Prof. B.: Very good! Please ask your teacher for an *E*-1 book and workbook. She'll help you get started. Read as much as you can and do at least the first workbook page that is assigned. See you for your next booklet.

Page 29

Prof. B.: Well, you did find the predicate, Freddy, so you're not incorrect. However, you were asked to find the whole predicate. "Sat" was just part of it.

Freddy: Oh. Let me try again.

Prof. B.: O. K. Turn back to Page 24.

Page 30

Prof. B.: And when you're told to turn to a page, what about all the pages that might be in between?

Freddy: I'm supposed to skip them and not peek at them.

Prof. B.: Is that what you did in the last booklet?

Freddy: I had to. When I tried to read the next page, I couldn't figure out what it was all about.

Prof. B.: It's really easy when you turn to the page you're told to. Right?

Freddy: Right. Say, Professor. What's a predicate?

Prof. B.: That's just what you're going to find out right now. Turn to Page 32.

Page 31

Prof. B.: Good work. "Ran" is the predicate because it comes at the end of a simple sentence, and it tells what the subject does or feels, or what the subject is like. Turn to Page 28.

Page 32

Prof. B.: Since a predicate is part of a sentence, let's have a little practice first with sentences. From the following groups of words, choose the sentence that makes sense. Your answer will tell you where to go.

Freddy: O. K.

Prof. B.: Remember. Some of these words make sense and some don't, but there's only one real *sentence* here that makes sense. You find it.

(a) The little girl. (Turn to Page 7.)
(b) The little girl broke her bicycle. (Turn to Page 9.)
(c) The broke her bicycle little girl. (Turn to Page 15.)
(d) The bicycle broke the little girl. (Turn to Page 16.)

Figure 11-2

TEACHER:

SUGGESTIONS FOR SUPPLEMENTARY LEARNING

R For remedial needs:	*Language for Daily Use* New Harbrace Edition Level Brown Mildred A. Dawson, Marian Zollinger, M. Ardell Elwell and Eric W. Johnson Harcourt Brace Jovanovich, Inc. New York, N.Y., 1973 Pages 25-27
	Workbook for the above Mildred A. Dawson, Marian Zollinger and K. Florence Morrissey Page 12
	Language and How to Use It Book 3 Andrew Schiller, Marion Monroe, Ralph Nichols, William Jenkins and Charlotte Huck Scott, Foresman and Company Glenview, Ill., 1973 Pages 61-66
E-1 For enrichment needs:	*Language and How to Use It* Book 3 (described above) Pages 118-19
	Language for Daily Use Level Brown (described above) Page 28
	Workbook for *Language for Daily Use* Level Brown Pages 14-16
E-2 For enrichment needs:	*Language for Daily Use* Level Brown (described above) Page 32

INDEX